Teach Yourself
VISUALLY™

Hand-Dyeing

Visual®

by Barbara Parry

WILEY

Wiley Publishing, Inc.

Praise for the Teach Yourself VISUALLY Series

I just had to let you and your company know how great I think your books are. I just purchased my third Visual book (my first two are dog-eared now!) and, once again, your product has surpassed my expectations. The expertise, thought, and effort that go into each book are obvious, and I sincerely appreciate your efforts. Keep up the wonderful work!

—Tracey Moore (Memphis, TN)

I have several books from the Visual series and have always found them to be valuable resources.

—Stephen P. Miller (Ballston Spa, NY)

Thank you for the wonderful books you produce. It wasn't until I was an adult that I discovered how I learn—visually. Although a few publishers out there claim to present the material visually, nothing compares to Visual books. I love the simple layout. Everything is easy to follow. And I understand the material! You really know the way I think and learn. Thanks so much!

—Stacey Han (Avondale, AZ)

Like a lot of other people, I understand things best when I see them visually. Your books really make learning easy and life more fun.

—John T. Frey (Cadillac, MI)

I am an avid fan of your Visual books. If I need to learn anything, I just buy one of your books and learn the topic in no time. Wonders! I have even trained my friends to give me Visual books as gifts.

—Illona Bergstrom (Aventura, FL)

I write to extend my thanks and appreciation for your books. They are clear, easy to follow, and straight to the point. Keep up the good work! I bought several of your books and they are just right! No regrets! I will always buy your books because they are the best.

—Seward Kollie (Dakar, Senegal)

Credits

Acquisitions Editor
Pam Mourouzis

Project Editor
Suzanne Snyder

Copy Editor
Catherine Schwenk

Technical Editors
Sara Lamb
Vicki Jensen

Editorial Manager
Christina Stambaugh

Publisher
Cindy Kitchel

Vice President and Executive Publisher
Kathy Nebenhaus

Interior Design
Kathie Rickard
Elizabeth Brooks

Photography
Matt Bowen

Additional Photography
Barbara Parry
Cynthia Herbert

About the Author

Barbara Parry raises sheep on her 220-acre farm in the Berkshire foothills of western Massachusetts. She dyes her own line of knitting yarn produced from the wool of her flock and markets it under her label, Foxfire Fiber and Designs, both online (at www.foxfirefiber.com) and at sheep and wool festivals throughout the Northeast. Her hand-dyed yarns and fibers have been featured in *Wild Fibers* magazine and in several knitting books. She chronicles life on her farm in her blog Sheep Gal (www.sheepgal.com) and is a free-lance writer contributing to fiber arts publications. She teaches classes in hand spinning, dyeing, and colorwork.

Acknowledgments

I thank the many people who contributed to this book: Pam Mourouzis, Suzanne Snyder, Matt Bowen, and the Wiley team; Vicki Jensen and Sara Lamb for their technical expertise and careful reading of my manuscript; Linda Roghaar; Kathy Elkins; knitwear designers Lisa Lloyd, Melissa Morgan Oakes, and Kirsten Hipsky; Barbara Giguere, Teresa Campbell, and Holly Sonntag, whose stitches composed the samples in the book; Holly Sonntag for reliable back-up at both the farm and studio; and the many friends and family members who helped in myriad ways. I especially thank my husband, Mike, whose encouragement and support made this project possible.

Table of Contents

chapter 1 **Why Learn to Dye?**

chapter 2 **A Dyer's Studio**

chapter 3 Different Dyes for Different Fibers

chapter 4 Yarn and Fiber Preparation

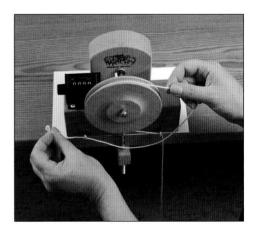

chapter 5 Work with Color

chapter 6 Immersion Dyeing

chapter 7 Hand-Paint Variations

chapter 8 Freestyle Dyeing

chapter 9 Dye Cellulose Fibers

chapter 10 Color on Color: The Artful Overdye

 **Spin and Knit with Hand-Dyed Fiber**

chapter **12** **Color Themes for Hand-Dyed Palettes**

Special thanks...

To the following companies for granting us permission to show photographs of their equipment:

KNITWEAR DESIGNS

Lisa Lloyd Designs
www.lloydknitting.com
Foxglove, p. 190
Patricia, pp. 197, 198
Road Not Taken, pp. 100, 188, 191
Vanilla Sock, pp. 98, 190
Vixen, p. 188

Melissa Morgan Oakes
www.melissaknits.com
Cable Motif, p. 175, 189
Country Garden Sock, p. 188

Webs
Designs by Kirsten Hipsky
Paradise City Pillow, pp. 153, 191
Stain Glass Purse, p. 191

COLOR TOOLS

The Color Wheel Company
Philomath, OR
www.colorwheelco.com
Color Wheel, pp. 41, 56, 59
Gray Scale Tool, p. 53

KNITTING NEEDLES AND SPINDLES

Grafton Fibers
Saxtons River, VT
www.graftonfibers.com

Additional photography by...

Photos courtesy of Barbara Parry, copyright Barbara Parry

Cover, Basket of Skeins
Border Leicester Ewe; Cormo Sheep, p. 22
Autumn Llama, p. 23
Dyer's Garden, p. 29
Mountain Sunrise, p. 63
Roadside Ferns; Spring Skeins, p. 64
Mason Jar Dye Skeins, p. 150

Autumn Skeins; Winter Sky Roving, p. 195
Lavender Harvest; Clover Field; Magnolia Blossom;
Tiger Lily, p. 197
Wool Locks; Woodland Skeins, p. 199
Sweet Potato Cormo Roving; Spice-Colored Silk;
Ginger Batts, p. 201

Photo courtesy of Cynthia Herbert, Keldaby Farm

Running Goat, p. 23

Why Learn to Dye?

Learning to dye fiber opens the door to an exciting new realm of color possibilities. Whether you knit, crochet, spin, weave, or felt, the greatest benefit of dyeing your own fiber is an unlimited range of color. The freedom of color choice in any fibers you wish to use presents a vast world of options.

My work with color in the dye pot began over a decade ago. I am fortunate to live on a 220-acre sheep farm in the Berkshire foothills of western Massachusetts. My flock provides an abundance of raw materials, and the ever-changing natural beauty of the pastoral landscape provides color inspiration.

Working with color on fiber is mesmerizing and addictive. This book will help you embark on your own color journey.

The Art and Alchemy of the Dyepot

Hand-dyeing is part art and part science. A dyer understands not only the use of color but also the process of creating color and pairing hues to create harmonious palettes. The art of dyeing requires a basic understanding of the chemical interaction of dye materials with fibers. A grasp of basic color principles also helps in the beginning.

Although you could spend years studying the complex chemistry that takes place in the dyeing process, by learning a few basic principles you can very quickly be on your way to achieving satisfying results in hand-dyed yarn and fiber.

This book introduces the basic technical information for using acid and fiber-reactive dyes on animal and plant fibers. Dyeing fibers is not hard, but it is important to understand how dyes work in order to use them safely and successfully.

I present a number of techniques for achieving different effects. Some methods involve preparing dye baths in large pots and submersing the fibers in them. Others involve various ways of directly applying color to the fiber to create a pattern.

I also present two different approaches to dyeing. If you are a systematic person who wants consistent, repeatable results, you will probably prefer the methods that require following formulas and using careful measurements. If you prefer spontaneity and a more freehand approach, you will enjoy the freestyle techniques. Either way, there is no right or wrong. Dyeing is fun, so just jump in and get started. The more you work with colors, the more comfortable you will become with the steps in the dye process.

Creativity drives all fiber artists. Knitters, spinners, felt makers, weavers, rug hookers—we all pursue our crafts for the joy that comes from creating something that is personal, unique, and one-of-a-kind. Color is central to design in any fiber project. Hand-dyeing gives you the freedom to create colorways in your own personal aesthetic. The added bonus is getting to work with fibers and yarns of your own choice.

Color Possibilities

Knitters are drawn by the magic of creating intricate designs one stitch at a time by working one continuous strand of yarn. Whether you are knitting a pair of socks or a cabled sweater, the ability to choose any yarn and dye it any color greatly expands your design options.

For hand-spinners, the range of choices becomes more exciting when you dye your own fibers for crafting yarn. There are many ways to achieve color effects in spinning.

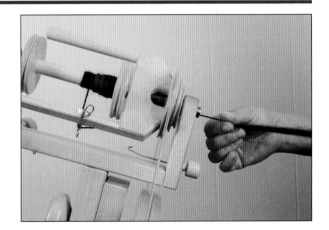

Weaving with hand-dyed yarn pushes the creative envelope further. Weavers can work magic by creating bold or subtle color effects at the loom. Hand-painted warps create exciting ikat-like stripes in scarves and runners. Semisolid yarns add depth and texture to clasped-weft designs.

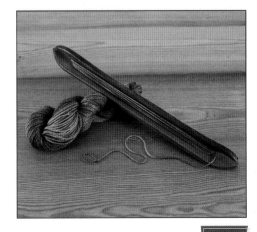

Fiber, Fiber Everywhere

The explosion of interest in fiber arts over the past decade has made a vast difference in the number of resources available to fiber artists. Classes, supplies, books, publications, websites, and support networks make it easier than ever to explore the craft of hand-dyeing. A quick surf of the Internet reveals a wide range of sources for dye materials. A few clicks of a mouse bring everything you need—dyes, dye assists, and all necessary paraphernalia—right to your door. (See the appendix for a list of online sources for dyeing supplies.)

The same holds true for procuring the raw materials for the dyer's craft—undyed fibers. With the fiber art surge, a class of online e-tailers has emerged, providing numerous sources of yarn, roving, and unprocessed fibers. Wool is available from just about every corner of the globe, from sheep of every imaginable breed. The variety of undyed yarn ranges from goat to yak to possum and everything in between. Plant fibers run the gamut from cotton to banana to bamboo. A relatively recent class of "green" fibers is now available for the organically inclined dyer. The appendix provides a list of online fiber suppliers.

Fiber festivals and local yarn stores bring the raw materials closer to home for many dyers. Purchasing fiber is a tactile experience, and hands-on shopping is the fastest way to determine your personal preferences. Buying fiber directly from a fiber farm enhances the special, unique quality of hand-crafted projects. It also supports the efforts of small-scale fiber producers and farm viability. (See the appendix for a listing of annual fiber shows and festivals.)

Opportunities for instruction, inspiration, and technical support in dyeing are everywhere. Major fiber-art print publications frequently include articles about hand-dyeing. Classes in dyeing are offered at many yarn stores and craft schools. A multitude of groups and websites are dedicated specifically to the topic of dyeing fiber. (See the appendix for a list of craft schools and online resources for instruction and support.)

One of the joys of dyeing is that you can start with some easy and basic techniques to familiarize yourself with the process and then quickly branch out. You will need a few basic tools, but you don't need a fancy dye studio to get started.

The joy of dyeing comes from having an unlimited color palette and the ability to create a wide range of effects with color on fiber. Hand-dyed yarns have subtleties and variations that give them character and set them apart from commercially produced yarns. They are truly one-of-a-kind. Once I began dyeing my own fibers ten years ago, I never looked at commercial yarns in the same way.

Here is an overview of methods described in this book:

Solid-Shade Dyeing

Semisolid Shades

Hand-Paint Methods

Special Effects

chapter 2

A Dyer's Studio

A dyer's studio doesn't need to be fancy to be efficient. Dyers work in their basements, garages, hobby rooms, and even kitchens—with certain precautions. The basic tools and equipment are commonly found household items or are readily available. You can easily and inexpensively set up a workspace and get started.

Tools, Equipment, and Supplies

You may already own many of the tools and items used in dyeing. Some items may be purchased inexpensively at discount stores, tag sales, or thrift shops. You need only a few basic items to get started.

Some of the dyes and chemicals used in the dye process are not easily found in stores. Fortunately, there are many online and catalog resources for purchasing specialized dye materials.

Equipment and Tools

TOOLS FOR MEASURING

You will need tools for liquid and dry measurements:

- Stainless steel or plastic measuring spoons
- Pyrex measuring cups in 2-cup and 4-cup sizes (500ml and 1,000ml, respectively)
- Graduated cylinders, plastic beakers, and plastic syringes
- A small kitchen or postal scale for weighing fiber
- A digital scale or triple-beam balance to accurately measure small amounts of dye powder (helpful, but not necessary if you do all your measuring with spoons)
- Weigh boats, or small plastic cups for weighing dye powder
- Grey spoons for measuring small amounts of dye for recipes (helpful, but not essential)
- A yardage counter for yarn
- A skein winder or an umbrella swift for winding yarn as it is measured

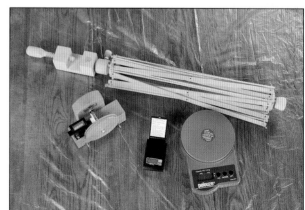

VESSELS FOR DYEING

It is helpful to have dye pots in a range of sizes to accommodate the size of particular projects. Forty-quart stockpots work well for large immersion dye baths of 1 pound or more. Twenty-quart pots are sufficient for variegated dyeing or smaller projects. The pots should either be made of stainless steel or have an unchipped enamel surface. Aluminum and iron will chemically interfere with the dye process.

For some projects, you can use a canning pot equipped with a rack. An inverted pie plate can be placed on the rack to create a chamber inside a pot for steaming plastic-wrapped packages of dyed yarn and roving. For slow-cooker dyeing, you will want to dedicate an electric slow cooker specifically for that purpose.

TOOLS FOR HANDLING FIBER AND STIRRING

For stirring dye baths and manipulating fiber, you need:

- Large wooden spoons and long-handled stainless-steel spoons
- Wooden dowels
- Bamboo rods or a rack for drying fiber
- White shoelaces for stringing skeins together in a soak or dye bath (Why white? White is easy to see and won't transfer color.)
- Large notebook rings for keeping dyed skeins organized
- Plastic shower curtain rings for handling dip-dyed skeins
- Mesh laundry bags for handling wool or mohair locks

CONTINUED ON NEXT PAGE

TOOLS FOR APPLYING COLOR

This book shows many different ways to apply color to yarn and fiber. The following items will come in handy, depending on which method you use:

- Foam brushes
- Short-bristle stencil brushes
- Plastic squeeze bottles
- Plastic syringes
- Spray bottles
- Plastic paint-mixing containers

COOKING EQUIPMENT

Many dyers cook right on their kitchen stoves. If your stove is electric, be sure to limit the weight of the pots you use; the weight of a heavy dye pot could crimp an electrical wire beneath the cooktop, causing a short. Be sure that burner sizes are appropriate for the size of pots, and never leave cooking dye pots unattended.

Several techniques in this book call for using a microwave oven. If you use a microwave oven for dyeing, it should no longer be used for preparing food.

Propane-fired outdoor cookers, such as the ones designed for boiling lobsters, are good for immersion dye projects outdoors. Be sure the burner stands on a level surface free from combustible materials and away from buildings. I do not suggest this approach on windy days. Keep children and pets away.

CHEMICALS AND DYE ASSISTS

The necessary auxiliary supplies depend on which dye process you use. You may purchase these items from the suppliers listed in the appendix.

- Dye powders
- *Synthrapol*, a pH-neutral surfactant used for soaking fibers and removing residual dye
- *Glauber salt*, a salt used instead of common table salt to level dyes
- *Citric acid crystals* or white vinegar (for acid dyes)
- Soda ash (for fiber-reactive dyes)
- *Urea*, used as a humectant with fiber-reactive dyes
- Dye thickeners, such as guar gum or Superclear
- Metaphos, a water softener (if you have hard water)

OTHER HELPFUL SUPPLIES

You may also need the following:

- Paper towels
- Sponges
- Newspapers (for covering surfaces)
- Plastic wrap
- Zipper-sealed plastic bags
- Vinyl or plastic table covers
- Plastic milk jugs with caps (for storing dye solutions)
- Undyed cotton string
- White coffee filter papers
- Pen and notepad

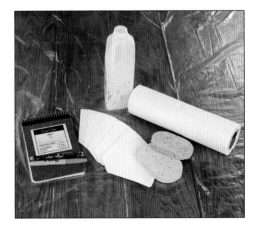

TIP

Warning

After a tool, vessel, or other piece of equipment has been used for dyeing, it should *never* be used for food preparation again. Label all dyeing tools clearly "FOR DYEING ONLY" so they are never accidentally used for food. Furthermore, you must never use dye materials while food is being prepared, and never eat or drink while dyeing. See the "Safety Essentials" section later in this chapter.

A Dyer's Workspace

Dyeing may initially seem like a messy process. If you are neat and take care to cover your work surfaces and clean up drips and spills quickly, you can avoid staining floors and work surfaces. You can dye in just about any room that has a sink and some type of cooking surface. My dyeing workspace is in my garage, with areas set aside for certain tasks.

My Workspace

I have a large three-basin sink that I use for wetting out fiber and filling pots. A small utility sink would suffice. A washing machine is conveniently located beside the sink for spinning out wet fiber.

I have two large cast-iron, propane-fired burners mounted to concrete blocks so they can't tip. The burners can support up to 60-quart pots, and I use them for kettle-dyeing yarn and fibers. This area has a strong exhaust fan for venting vapors.

I do most of my work at a large table adjacent to the sink. A vinyl tablecloth makes this surface easy to clean between projects. Windows provide good natural light, and overhead fluorescent lighting eliminates shadows. My storage shelves are nearby, so everything I need is within reach.

At the other side of the room, there are drying racks and bamboo rods for hanging yarn and roving to dry. I use fans and a dehumidifier to speed drying time.

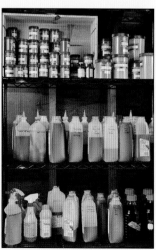

Thoughts When Creating a Workspace

While a look at a working studio is helpful to get a sense of the equipment needed, in the beginning, you are not likely to have a workspace dedicated solely to dyeing. Remember that you never want to mix the activities of food preparation, eating, drinking, or smoking with dyeing. I realize that many of you may dye in the kitchen, so I emphasize the importance of this.

Wherever you work, good ventilation is important during the cooking/steaming part of the job. Even when wearing a respirator cartridge mask (see the "Safety Essentials" section that follows), it is important to allow the vapors and odors to escape from the room.

Note: The only time you do not want air movement is when handling dye powders and other materials in powder or crystal form. Chapter 5 goes into more detail about safely mixing dye powders.

Make sure you cover your work surface with an easy-to-clean vinyl table covering, and keep sponges and paper towels handy.

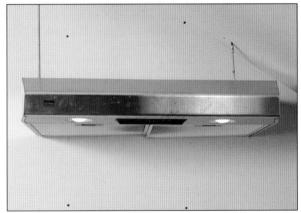

Dyeing outdoors is a great way to avoid creating a mess inside. If you are using an outdoor burner, be sure it is away from buildings and vehicles, and set it on a stable surface such as a concrete patio. Make sure there are no combustible materials such as leaves or grass nearby. Keep children and pets away. Do not attempt to dye outdoors on a windy day.

Safety Essentials

Dyeing is a fun, creative process, yet dyers must take safety seriously. Dye materials are safe to use as long as you follow the supplier's instructions and some basic precautionary guidelines. The misuse or mishandling of dyes and materials used in dyeing could lead to harmful results such as allergic reactions if the dye comes in contact with your skin or if you inhale dye powder. If you are pregnant or lactating, consult the dye supplier regarding safety.

PROTECT YOUR SKIN

Wear rubber, latex, or nitrile gloves when mixing dye solutions or when adding substances like salt or acid crystals to a dye bath. When hand-painting yarn, protect your hands from direct contact with liquid dye. If you do get dye stains on your hands or fingernails, you can use a special hand cleanser called ReDuRan (available from dye suppliers) to remove it.

When working with a simmering dye bath, wear insulated thermal gloves designed especially for dyers. Use hot mitts when handling hot cooking tools.

Sometimes you soak fibers in a citric acid or alkaline solution before dyeing. These solutions are caustic and will sting if the liquid gets on your skin. Wear long gloves to protect your hands and arms.

PROTECT YOUR LUNGS

When mixing dye powders into solutions, there is great risk of dye powder molecules becoming airborne. Since acid dyes have an affinity for protein and human bodies are largely comprised of proteins, you must reduce your exposure to dye in all forms, but especially in powdered form. Wear a particle filter mask whenever handling dye powders or any powdered dye material. You should also wear a dual cartridge respirator mask filled with acid gas cartridges to protect your lungs from irritation caused by the acid vapors of simmering dye baths. Check with your dye supply company to be sure you use the correct type of mask.

When mixing dye powders, turn off fans and close windows to avoid air movement. Cover your work surface with paper towels, and lightly dampen the paper with water from a spray bottle to trap any loose dye particles that spill before they become airborne. You also can create a mixing box lined with dampened paper. (This technique is explained in Chapter 5.) When cooking your dye baths, good ventilation is important. Turn on vent fans and open a window.

PROTECT YOUR EYES

Wear safety glasses to protect your eyes whenever you are working in the dye studio.

SAFETY SUMMARY

Safety Checklist

- Apron
- Rubber, latex, or nitrile gloves
- Insulated gloves
- Disposable particle mask
- Dual cartridge respirator mask filled with acid gas cartridges
- Safety glasses

Safety Practices

- Never use your dyeing tools for food preparation. Label all tools DYE USE ONLY so no one will ever mistakenly use them for another purpose.
- Never eat, drink, or prepare food while you are dyeing.
- Keep children and pets out of the room while dyeing and store all dyeing products out of reach of children and pets.
- Follow supplier instructions for dye products, which may vary.
- When storing unused dye solutions, be sure to label containers clearly (especially if reusing beverage containers) and store them well out of reach of children.
- Keep your workspace free from clutter and tripping hazards.
- Take care when lifting large heavy pots of water. Never attempt to move a heated dye bath. Use pot holders if you must adjust the position of a dye pot.
- Wear insulated gloves, safety glasses, and a respirator mask when stirring or manipulating fibers in the dye pot.
- Always allow fibers to cool completely before handling.

Storage and Disposal

Dyes and materials associated with dyeing should be stored in a cool, dry space out of direct sunlight and out of reach of children. Airtight containers should be use for storing all powders and liquids. Always replace lids tightly after using dye powders and chemicals.

Storage

Be sure all items are labeled clearly, also marking the date purchased or mixed. Use plastic rather than glass jars for storing liquid dyes, since breakage would cause quite a mess. Empty plastic milk jugs make great dye storage containers.

Various dyes and dye products have different shelf lives. You should check with your dye supplier to find out what the shelf life is for individual products and inquire about safe disposal.

Dye solutions made from acid dye powders (such as PRO Chem's WashFast or Cushing dyes) can be stored in plastic containers for up to six months, as long as acid has not been added to the dye solution.

Some colors tend to thicken and some tend to separate when stored. Sometimes stirring or heating a dye stock that has solidified will render it usable. It is always best to test a solution using a fiber sample when using a dye solution that has been sitting for a while.

Fiber-reactive dye solutions do not store well for long periods. It is important to prepare only as much dye as you will use. Leftover reactive dyes from hand-painting projects are usable within 5 days of mixing.

Disposal

An efficient dyer uses only the necessary amount of dye for a specific project. If you use your dye solutions judiciously, there should be very little, if any, dye left over for disposal. Leftover acid dyes can be used in various ways. If you have *unexhausted dye* (dye that has not fixed on the fiber) left in an acid dye bath, use it to dye leftover bits of wool locks or small amounts of yarn that can be incorporated into other projects. I buy and keep on hand blank silk scarves (see the appendix for suppliers) and drop them into unexhausted dye baths to soak up the remaining dye molecules. This way, I have matching hand-dyed silk scarves to accompany hand-knit sweaters.

When you are completely finished with an acid dye bath, you should neutralize the bath. Add baking soda 1 tablespoon at a time and use pH test papers to verify that the exhausted bathwater is neutralized. Then pour the exhausted dye bath down the drain, flushing with plenty of water.

Disposing of unexhausted fiber-reactive dye baths is less simple. You can't use any leftover dye that the yarn hasn't absorbed because the dye molecules have actually *hydrolized* (bonded with the water molecules) and therefore can no longer bond with fiber. If you have unexhausted dye in the pot, you must balance the pH. A fiber-reactive dye bath is basic; add citric acid crystals 1 tablespoon at a time until you have brought the bath to a neutral pH before disposal. Check the supplier's instructions for the safest method of disposal. Some dye companies suggest pouring the neutralized bath down the drain, using plenty of water. If you have a bath with a lot of leftover dye, another option is to store it in plastic jugs. Most communities have clean-up days where they will collect household chemicals. Be sure you label the contents of the containers.

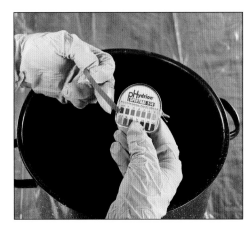

3

Different Dyes for Different Fibers

Yarns and fibers available today are derived from a wide variety of sources. They can be grouped into two main categories for the purpose of dyeing: *protein fibers* (from animals) and *cellulose fibers* (from plants). Each type of fiber has its own structure and chemical composition. An understanding of fiber basics will help you choose the correct dye and the right process for working with specific fibers.

This book demonstrates the use of two classes of synthetic dye most commonly used by home dyers and small-scale production dyers: *acid dyes* for protein fibers and *fiber-reactive dyes* for cellulose fibers. These dyes are readily available and are easy and safe to use.

Protein fibers, primarily the fibers grown on the backs of animals, are composed of specific combinations of amino acids which vary from species to species. This class of fiber covers a wide range of animals—from sheep to yak—but also includes silk, which comes from the secretions of the silkworm.

Sources of Protein Fiber

SHEEP

The wide variety of sheep raised throughout the world produce an incredible range of wool fibers. Whether you are dyeing merino yarn or the locks of a longwool breed, the underlying characteristics of wool dictate the same class of dye. Fleeces can be white, but they also come in a wide range of natural colors. Overdyeing a colored fleece adds depth to the color (see Chapter 10).

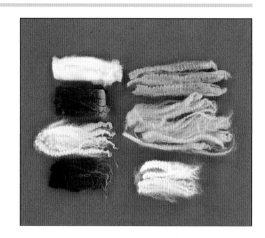

Wool fibers are made of a protein called *keratin* and are covered with a series of overlapping scales called the *cuticle*. In order to evenly dye wool, the dye must fully penetrate the cuticle. Scouring wool fleeces and wetting out the fiber using Synthrapol aid in preparing wool to accept dye (see Chapter 4). During the dye process, the scales of wool fibers can become locked together if you handle the fiber too vigorously when wet. This process is called *felting* and it is irreversible.

The length of the wool staple and cuticle scales varies depending on the sheep breed. *Staple length* is the length of a natural lock of wool fiber. The longer the scales, the more shiny the wool appears. Border Leicester and Cotswold are longwool breeds with lustrous fleeces. Fine wool breeds, such as Merino and Cormo, have a shorter staple length and the cuticle scales are shorter and closer together. Handle fine wools with extra care in dyeing since they tend to felt more easily.

Border Leicester, a longwool breed

Cormo, a fine wool breed

FAQ

What is superwash wool?

Superwash wool has been treated in a process that either smoothes down the scales on the outer layer of wool fiber or coats them with a polymer substance. The process enables the wool to be machine washed without felting. Acid dyes are used on superwash wool fibers.

GOATS

The glossy, long fiber known as *mohair* comes from Angora goats. The surface of mohair fiber is composed of long scales that reflect light, giving it an amazing sheen. *Cashmere,* an incredibly fine, soft fiber produced by Cashmere goats, is quite short in staple length and does not have a sheen. Its delicate nature means it must be handled carefully in the dyeing process. Cashmere roving can drift apart when wet and also felts easily.

*Photo by Cynthia Herbert,
Keldaby Farm*

CAMELIDS

This class of fiber comes from llamas, alpacas, camels, vicuna, and guanaco. There is a range of fiber length. Some camelids are dual coated—which means that they have undesirable guard hairs mixed within their soft, downy fleeces. Guard hair is coarse and does not accept dye. When camelid fiber is processed, the guard hairs are removed by a procedure called *dehairing*.

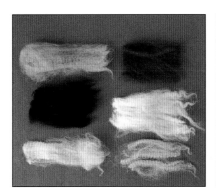

ANGORA RABBITS

There are several breeds of Angora rabbits, raised especially for their fine, soft fiber. The soft fur is harvested by combing, clipping, or plucking and is highly prized by knitters and spinners. Angora is easy to dye, but must be handled carefully when wet to avoid felting. It is often used in blends with other fibers.

CONTINUED ON NEXT PAGE

SILKWORMS

Silk fiber is created by the secretion of the silkworm when it spins a cocoon. It has an incredible sheen and can be dyed with either acid or fiber-reactive dyes. Silk's special nature requires careful attention to temperature (not to exceed 185°F) when using acid dyes.

A gummy substance called *sericin* holds silk cocoons together. This is removed in a process called *degumming* when the fiber is made into roving or yarn. A thorough presoak in a warm bath with Synthrapol removes sericin traces and prepares silk fiber to evenly accept dye (see Chapter 4).

Different types of caterpillar produce different types of silk. The Bombyx Mori caterpillar produces Bombyx silk, also called *cultivated silk* because the caterpillars are hand-raised and fed mulberry leaves. White cultivated silk yields the brightest colors when dyed. *Muga* and *tussah*, often called "wild silks," come from caterpillars that feed on a variety of trees, including oak. The tannins in the leaves give wild silk a honey color that adds depth when dyed.

SOY SILK

Soy silk is the trade name for fiber produced from the soybean. (It is actually a byproduct of tofu manufacturing.) The fiber is extruded from a soy paste. It has the lustrous appearance of silk and comes in a natural honey color or in a bleached white. While technically a plant fiber, soy silk is comprised of proteins and can be dyed with acid dyes.

FAQ

What about exotics?

This category includes the fiber from musk ox, known as *qiviut,* as well as the fiber from yak and possum. While many of the fibers in this class are naturally colored, they can be overdyed for interesting results. *Overdyeing* is the process of dyeing on top of a fiber that has a natural base color (see Chapter 10).

WEAK ACID DYES

The projects in this book use PRO Chem's WashFast and Cushing's Perfection Dyes, which are *weak acid dyes*. A weak acid dye requires a mild acidity (a pH in the range of 4–6) for the chemical bond between dye and fiber to occur.

In *immersion dyeing* (the process of immersing fibers in a heated dye bath for a set amount of time), you add acid—either citric acid crystals or white vinegar—to the dye bath (see Chapter 6). In direct application dyeing, you alter the pH of the fibers by soaking them in a mild solution of acid, Synthrapol, and water. Then you apply the dye in the technique of your choice (see Chapter 7). Either way, acid and heat are necessary for the dye process to occur. In immersion dyeing, Glauber salt is used to level the dye bath. It slows the dye process, giving time for even color distribution.

OPPOSITES ATTRACT

What actually happens between dye molecules and fiber molecules during the dye process? In acid dyeing, dye and fiber become united by a chemical process called an *ionic bond*. Neutral protein fiber molecules link with positively charged acid ions in the dye bath. The positively charged wool-acid sites on the fiber attract the dye molecules, which are negatively charged. The result is an ionic bond with the acid serving as a link.

OTHER TYPES OF ACID DYES

Some acid dyes, such as PRO Chem's One Shot or Gaywool's Country Colors, do not require the addition of citric acid or vinegar. These dyes come premixed with acid grains or crystals, which makes them very easy for beginners to use. Kool-Aid can be used as a "one-step" dye since the beverage powder contains dye and citric acid crystals. Chapters 6 and 8 include projects with "one-step" dyes.

Note: *There is another class of acid dyes, called* leveling dyes, *which are not used in this book. These dyes require stronger acids and slightly different processes.*

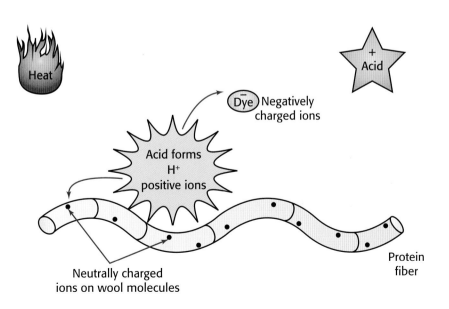

Fiber-Reactive Dyes for Cellulose Fibers

The chemistry of plant fibers requires a different type of dye process. Plant fibers are made of cellulose, which is a complex carbohydrate that will not bond with acid dye.

Types of Cellulose Fibers

COTTON

Cotton is produced from the fiber harvested from the bolls of cotton plants. Although cotton is typically white or off-white, there are growers producing naturally colored cotton. A good pre-scouring is required when dyeing cotton fiber. In mercerized cotton, the fiber surface has been smoothed. It is shiny in appearance and accepts dye more readily than minimally processed cotton fiber.

BAST AND OTHER FIBERS

Other common cellulose fibers include flax, hemp, ramie, and jute, which come from the stalks of plants and are known as *bast fibers.* Bamboo is another popular cellulose fiber, often found alone or in wool blends.

MAN-MADE CELLULOSE FIBERS

Rayon and *Tencel* (a trademark name for the fiber lyocell) are examples of man-made cellulose fibers. Cellulose is extruded to produce a filament for spinning into yarn. Although the material is natural, the fibers themselves are engineered.

How Fiber-Reactive Dyes Work

Since the chemical composition of cellulose fibers is different from the chemical composition of protein fibers, a different class of dye is needed. Molecules of fiber-reactive dye contain reactive sites that bond directly with sites on cellulose fibers. The bond that is created is called a *covalent bond,* and it is stronger than the ionic bond that occurs in acid dyeing. In a covalent bond, the two materials actually share electrons. This bond is extremely washfast.

Fiber-reactive dyes can be used in either immersion or direct application dye processes. Both methods are shown in Chapter 9. Alkalinity is necessary for the chemical bond to take place between reactive dyes and fiber. Soda ash assists in the dye process by raising the pH to 10.5 either in a dye bath for immersion dyeing or in an alkaline presoak for direct application dyeing. Heat is not needed for the chemical bond to occur when using PRO MX-reactive dye, which is used in Chapter 9. Cibracon/ Sabracon F is another widely used reactive dye (not demonstrated in this book). It is similar to the PRO MX dye, but works at a slightly warmer temperature. In immersion dyeing with reactive dyes, salt is used as a leveling agent, giving the dye time to evenly penetrate the fibers before becoming permanently fixed.

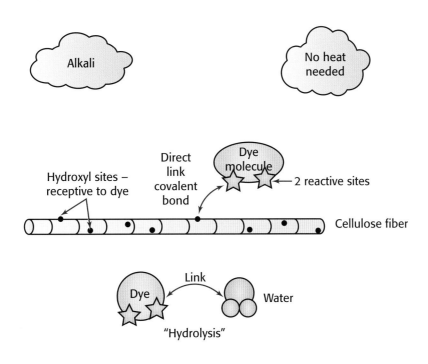

Dyeing Fiber Blends

Fiber blends enhance the unique qualities of two or more different fibers. Working with them is exciting, but they sometimes pose challenges for dyers. In order to dye blends successfully, you need to know a little about the component fibers and the dyes that work best for them. Because different fibers take dye differently, it is a good idea to sample before dyeing a large quantity of blended fibers.

PROTEIN FIBER BLENDS

Many different combinations of protein fibers are available. In general, the same acid dye processes you would use for any protein fiber will work for blends. You must take special care of any blends containing silk. Never allow the temperature to exceed 185°F when working with silk blends.

If your fiber blend includes fibers that are fine, delicate, or short, take extra care in handling them when wet.

NYLON BLENDS

Nylon fiber is often used as a core or binder in bouclé or brushed yarns. Wool sock yarns often contain a percentage of nylon for resiliency and strength. Fortunately, the chemical structure of nylon is similar to protein fiber, therefore acid dyes can be used for these blends.

CELLULOSE FIBER BLENDS

Blends of cellulose fiber are not as common as protein fiber blends. Because the properties of all-cellulose fibers are similar, fiber-reactive dyes work for blends of plant fibers.

WHAT ABOUT PROTEIN/CELLULOSE BLENDS?

Blends comprised of animal and plant fibers, such as merino and bamboo or merino and Tencel, are quite popular, but they present a challenge for dyers since the chemical structure of the component fibers is quite different. There is no ideal method for addressing both fibers at once. Acid dyes do not work on cellulose fibers. Fiber-reactive dyes *can* be used on protein fibers (with the addition of acid and heat), but this process doesn't address the cellulose half of the blend. Dyeing wool or other protein fibers using reactive dyes in an alkaline approach can quite easily damage the protein fiber. (Silk is the exception here.)

One answer to the dilemma is to use the process you would ordinarily use for the fiber that makes up the higher percentage of the blend. For example, if a blend is 80% wool and 20% bamboo, use an acid dye. The wool portion of the blend will be a solid color, while the bamboo portion of the blend will have a somewhat heathered appearance.

If the blend is a 50/50 mix of plant and animal fiber, I suggest testing before dyeing. Run a small test batch with acid dye. Run a second test batch with reactive dye. Neither batch will have a completely solid color, but you can determine which result is more pleasing. You can see how well the fiber held up to the dye process.

A third option is to try a two-step process. Address the animal fiber component in an acid dye bath. Then overdye the fiber, using reactive dyes to dye the plant component of the blend. This process works best with blends containing superwash wool, which is better able to withstand the harsh alkalinity used in reactive dyeing.

UNION DYES

Union dyes are all-purpose catch-alls designed to work with a wide range of fibers. A union dye contains the materials to dye both protein and the cellulose fibers as well as some synthetic fibers. The instructions for using these dyes vary, based on the type of fiber. Because the dye contains material for both types of fiber, some of the material will be wasted, since only half the material will be used based on which type of fiber is being dyed. Union dyes are widely available, easy to use, and inexpensive, but their color permanence may vary.

NATURAL DYES

For centuries before the development of man-made dyes, plant and other natural materials were used to dye fibers. *Natural dyes* are produced from plants with known dye properties. Marigolds, cosmos, onion skins, lichen, and black walnuts are examples of plant material that yield color for natural dyeing. Other sources of natural colors include cochineal bugs, which produce a bright red. In order to get the dye to bond with the fiber, chemical assistants called *mordants* are used to enable the plant material to interact with the fibers. Fibers are treated in a mordant bath before the natural dyestuff is added. By using different mordants, different colors can be achieved from the same plant materials. Because many traditionally used mordants contain toxic heavy metals (such as tin or chrome), they pose health and environmental risks. Today, many natural dyers use food-grade alum as a safer alternate mordant.

chapter 4

Yarn and Fiber Preparation

Whether you are dyeing yarn, roving, or raw fleece, proper fiber preparation is essential for good results. The two basic steps in preparing dye goods are arranging the fibers in a manner that will make handling easy throughout the dyeing process and wetting out the fibers so the dyes can penetrate and adhere evenly.

Wind and Tie Yarn Skeins

Yarn must be wound into neat, well-tied skeins to prevent it from tangling and to allow even distribution of dye liquid in the dye process. Undyed yarns may come on cones, in center-pull balls, or in pull skeins that can easily come undone. Use a skein winder or an umbrella swift to create dye skeins.

Wind Skeins

In the beginning it is easiest to work with skeins that are a manageable size of approximately 250 yards with a 2-yard circumference. Regardless of the number of yards, you will also need to know the weight of the skeins to calculate the right amount of dye. Yarn and fiber being dyed are referred to as *dye goods,* and the weight of yarn or fiber being dyed is called the *weight of goods.*

You need a skein winder or an umbrella swift and a yardage counter, if you wish to know the exact yardage of the skein before dyeing. Keep in mind there will be fiber shrinkage during the dye process. A skein may decrease in yardage (but not necessarily in weight) during dyeing. The amount of shrinkage depends on the type of fiber. You will also need scissors and thin cotton string for making ties.

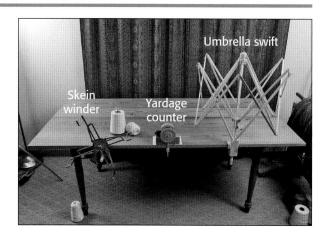

1 Clamp the skein winder or umbrella swift to one end of a work table. Extend the arms of the winder (or the ribs of the swift) to a circumference of approximately 2 yards.

2 Position the yardage counter at least 18 inches away from the winder and clamp it to the table. Placing the cone of yarn on the floor to the right of the yardage counter, feed the yarn through the guides on the counter. Be sure to set the counter to zero before winding.

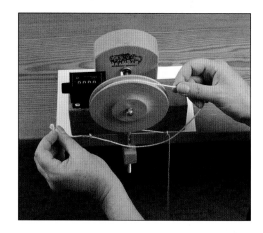

3 Tie the yarn to the end of one arm of the skein winder (or fasten to one rib of the swift). When you turn the handle of the winder or spin the swift, the yarn will run through the counter and onto the winder. Stop when you have reached your desired yardage, but stop in a place where both ends of the skein meet.

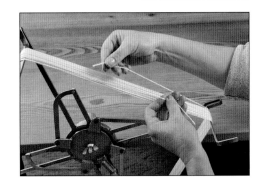

Tie Skeins

4 To secure the skein, take one end and wrap it around the entire bundle of yarn. Then bring the end through the loop you have just created. Do the same with the other end. Then join both ends with a secure knot. When securing both ends of the skein, wrap the skein loosely to prevent forming a resist.

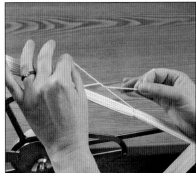

5 To prevent tangling, put at least three loose figure-8 ties in the skein. To make a tie, take a 6-inch piece of string and, dividing the bundle of yarn in half, wrap the string around the yarn bundle. Crisscross the ends of the string and wrap around the second bundle of yarn. While keeping this figure-8 wrap loose, tie a secure knot. A loose figure-8 tie will allow the dye to flow freely through the yarn strands while keeping the skein in order.

Ready Roving

Handling wet roving can be tricky since the weight of wet fiber tends to pull the roving apart. Making neat bundles of roving makes handling much easier. You must know the weight of roving in order to prepare the correct amount of dye.

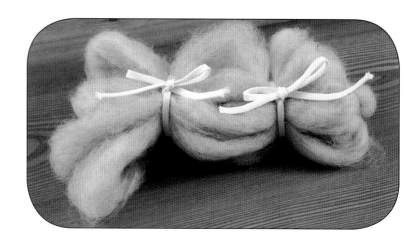

Make a Roving Bundle

When learning to dye, it's easier to manage smaller amounts of roving. Two-ounce hanks are a good place to start. A kitchen or postal scale is convenient for weighing fiber in small increments.

Take the length of roving and fold it in half. Then fold it in half twice more and place it on a table. Use two 6-inch lengths of white shoelace or string to loosely secure the roving at both ends.

FAQ

What are roving and top?

Roving and *top* are two slightly different fiber preparations used to spin different types of yarn. Roving (A) is produced by carding fibers, and top (B) is made from combed fibers. In roving, the fibers are randomly aligned and the preparation is light and airy. Roving is less dense than top and therefore takes less time to wet out the fiber. In top, the fibers are dense and parallel in arrangement. It takes longer to wet out top, and top also can require more dye. While technically incorrect, the word *roving* is often applied to both. For dyeing purposes, you handle them both in the same manner.

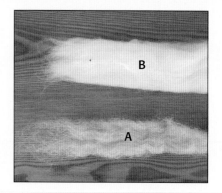

Dyed locks of fleece are said to be *dyed in the wool*. If you have a raw fleece, (as shown here) you should first wash it to remove some of the lanolin and dirt it accumulated while worn by a sheep. While it is possible to *dye in the grease* (which means dyeing unwashed wool), you will have better results if you give it a simple scour. The wool will not be squeaky clean, but a sufficient amount of dirt and grease will be removed to enable a good dye bond.

Scour the Wool

For purposes of dyeing, I have found that a three-soak bath sufficiently removes enough grime to ensure fairly even dye absorption.

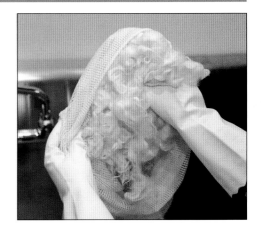

1 Divide the fleece into manageable amounts, placing roughly 8–12 ounces of wool into mesh laundry bags. Fill a wash basin with hot (110°F) water to which you have added ½ teaspoon of Synthrapol. Place no more than two bags of fiber into the bath at once. Gently press to submerge, but DO NOT AGITATE. Allow the wool to soak for no more than 3 minutes.

2 Fill a second basin with 130 to 140°F water. Add ½ teaspoon Synthrapol and submerge the wool bag. Remove the bag after a three-minute soak. Be sure to wear insulated rubber gloves as the water is hot.

3 Fill a third basin with 110°F water, but no Synthrapol. Transfer the fiber bags to the third bath and allow them to soak for an additional 5 minutes.

4 Repeat this process until you have scoured the remaining wool. Place the bags on a rack so the water can drain, then remove the fiber and spread it on a rack to dry.

5 Once the fiber has thoroughly dried, gently pick apart the locks of wool with your hands. Opening up the fleece enables the dye to penetrate more evenly.

Wet Out the Fiber

With a few exceptions, all fibers, whether yarn, roving, or wool locks, should be presoaked before dyeing. This process is called *wetting out the fiber*, and it does two things: It removes any spinning oil or residual dirt that may inhibit dye uptake; and the Synthrapol breaks the surface tension of the water, making it easier to saturate the fiber completely before dyeing. This facilitates the bond between dye molecules and fiber.

THE PRESOAK

1. Add ½ teaspoon Synthrapol to a sink or basin of water. The temperature of the water should be room temperature to warm (95°F or 35°C) depending on the fiber and the process.

2. Place the yarn or fiber in the presoak for a minimum of 30 minutes, sometimes more, depending on the fiber.

3. After removing the fiber from the soak, gently extract the excess water. The spin cycle on your washing machine will spin out enough moisture after 1 minute to leave sufficient moisture in the fiber for dyeing. Make sure you turn off the water so you don't add more water as you spin!

Note: A salad spinner is a handy tool for spinning water out of small amounts of yarn or fiber. This is helpful if you are dyeing small sample skeins.

TIPS FOR WETTING OUT FIBER

- To keep yarn skeins from tangling in the soak and during immersion dyeing, loop a piece of shoelace or string through all skeins. This leash will keep the skeins together and prevent them from tangling.

- Handle wet roving very carefully. Never agitate wet roving as this may cause the fibers to *felt* (lock together). Always use two hands when lifting a hank of roving from the presoak, being sure to support the mass of fiber.

- Wool locks are easier to handle if they are placed in a mesh laundry bag. Be careful not to agitate wool locks because they can also felt.

- Certain fibers take longer to wet out. Silk generally needs to soak for at least an hour. Tightly twisted yarns and densely compressed top may also require more time.

MAKING AN ACID PRESOAK FOR PROTEIN FIBERS

Some dye procedures require that you add acid to the presoak. Soaking fibers in an acid bath makes them receptive to the dyes by altering the fibers' pH. This type of soak is used most often for direct application techniques. Soak fibers for at least thirty minutes before dyeing. Here's how to make an acid presoak for 1 pound/454g of fiber:

1. Use a 5-gallon plastic bucket with a lid. Add 6 tablespoons citric acid crystals and 2 teaspoons Synthrapol to 1 gallon room-temperature water (approximately 95°F/35°C).

2. Store the acid soak for future dye projects by placing a tight lid on the bucket.

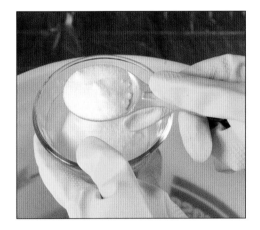

CREATING AN ALKALINE PRESOAK FOR CELLULOSE FIBERS

When using direct-application technique on cellulose fibers, you must soak them in an alkaline presoak for 15 minutes prior to dyeing. This changes the alkalinity of the fibers so they will bond with the dye.

1. Use a 5-gallon plastic bucket with a lid. Add 9 tablespoons of soda ash to 1 gallon warm water.

2. When finished, place a tight-fitting lid on the bucket and store for future use.

Note: Wear rubber glove and safety glasses when handling fibers in acid and alkaline soaks.

chapter 5

Work with Color

Dyers approach color work in different ways. Some work intuitively, while others prefer a systematic approach that relies on exact measurement and color theory. Some dyers use a little of both approaches. Whether you dye by numbers or dye by eye, an understanding of how colors interact and how to formulate colors is a helpful foundation. Working with color is pure joy. There is no right or wrong. The best way to get started is to jump right in.

The color wheel is a dyer's navigational tool. Whether you are mixing colors or planning a color palette for hand-dyed fiber, having an understanding of how to use this helpful tool will make your work easier. The color wheel shows the position of colors' relationships to one another. Knowledge of the geography of color will take you where you want to go in dyeing.

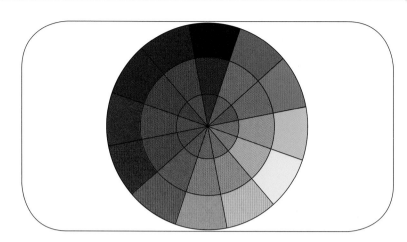

The *primary colors* red, blue, and yellow are the main points on the color-wheel and the building blocks for all other colors. Primary colors are pure. All other colors are formed by mixing these colors in varying proportions. Blend any two primary colors in equal amounts to create *secondary colors*: orange, green, and purple.

Secondary colors lie half way between the primary colors on the colorwheel.

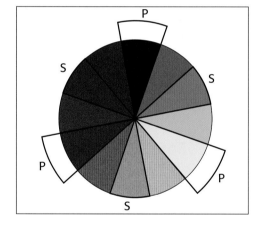

More complex colors are created by blending a primary color with an adjacent secondary color. *Tertiary colors* lie between primary and secondary colors on the color wheel. They are formed by mixing a primary color with a secondary color:

    Red + Orange = Red/Orange
    Yellow + Orange = Yellow/Orange
    Yellow + Green = Yellow/Green
    Blue + Green = Blue/Green
    Blue + Purple = Blue/Purple
    Red + Purple = Red/Purple

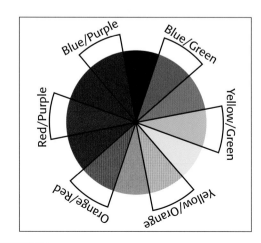

A color wheel is divided into two hemispheres based on the temperature of colors. How do colors have temperature? When we think of heat, we picture the colors of fire and the sun: reds, oranges, and yellows. These colors form the warm side of the color wheel. Blues and greens are the colors of water, the sky, or a shady lawn. They are considered cool colors. A line divides the cool and warm sides of the color wheel.

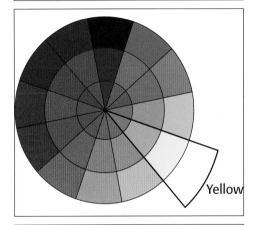

The colors at the outer rim of a color wheel tool are pure hues. (*Hue* is another word for color.) The slice highlighted in the diagram shows the hue family yellow. A hue family is comprised of a pure hue and the tints and shades that make up a range of values for that hue. Tints are lighter values and shades are deeper values of the original color.

Look at the hue family and you will see the colors become more subdued as you move toward the center of the wheel. Adding a bit of a color's complement dampens the original color. A color's *complement* is the hue that lies on the opposite side of the wheel. Red and green are complementary colors, as they lie opposite one another on the color wheel. Blue's complement is orange; purple is the complement of yellow. As the percentage of a complement increases, the original color becomes duller. The dampened versions of the original color are called *shades. (Illustration courtesy of the Color Wheel Company.)*

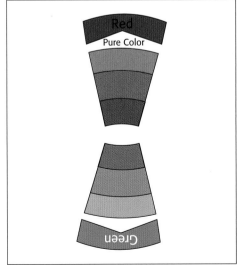

CONTINUED ON NEXT PAGE

A color's *saturation* (also called *intensity*) refers to the purity or clarity of hue. Imagine a white sponge absorbing a glass of spilled fruit punch. If you tried to sponge up the entire glass at once, the sponge would be completely saturated, dripping with liquid, and would be the same bright color as the punch. Colors have degrees of saturation. *Saturation* describes how bright or dull a color appears. A color is less saturated when it has been subdued by adding degrees of its complement to form a less intense hue.

As mentioned earlier, the color wheel has a cool side and a warm side. Each color also has its own temperature. Take purple, the secondary color formed by mixing equal amounts of red and blue. On one side of purple—going toward blue—there is violet, a purplish hue. Because violet leans toward the cool side of the color wheel (the blue/green side), its temperature is cooler than purple.

Now look at the hue on the other side of purple, which tilts toward red on the warmer side of the color wheel. This purple hue is "warmed" by the addition of red.

Understanding the position and relationship of hues on the color wheel and how value, saturation, and temperature influence a color's appearance takes a little practice. The exercises in this chapter help to ground you in the basics of color theory as it relates to dyeing. You will learn the basic steps in creating dye solutions and how to blend primary colors to create new colors.

It's easier and safer to work with dyes in liquid form, whether you are using acid or fiber-reactive dyes. Because inhaling dye powder poses a risk, mixing it with water to form *dye stocks* (also called *dye solutions*) makes color mixing safer. Liquid dye stock is also easier to measure using plastic syringes, beakers, and graduated cylinders.

Acid dye solutions are prepared with boiling water. Fiber-reactive dye solutions are generally mixed at room temperature. Acid dye stocks can be stored and used later. Reactive dyes have a shorter shelf life once mixed (see Chapter 9).

TOOLS AND MATERIALS

You need the following tools and materials for mixing dye stock:

- 4-cup (1,000ml) Pyrex measuring cup
- Measuring spoons
- Digital scale
- Small spoons or stirring sticks
- Boiling water (for acid dyes)
- Room-temperature water (for fiber-reactive dyes)
- Powdered dye
- Sponges
- Paper towels
- Dye mixing box (see Tip on page 44)

SAFETY

Take every precaution to avoid inhaling dye powder. Always wear a new dust particle mask for each mixing session. Minimize air movement (close windows, turn off fans) while measuring and mixing. Replace lids firmly on dye powder jars immediately after measuring. Wear rubber gloves and safety glasses, and keep children and pets out of your workspace. Never eat or drink while preparing dyes. Label all stock solutions clearly.

CONTINUED ON NEXT PAGE

Create a Dye Solution

MIX DYE STOCK

Carefully measure the desired amount of dye powder and place it in the Pyrex measuring cup. You may either use measuring spoons or a scale to measure dye powder (see page 45). Slowly add 2 tablespoons of boiling water (for acid dyes) and mix the dye to form a paste. Some dye powders are dry and sticky at first. Others form curds when water is added. It's important to mix the paste until it is completely smooth before adding more water.

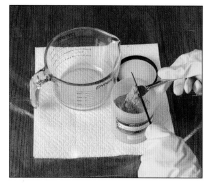 

Slowly add water to make the total amount of solution desired. Stir continuously until all the dye particles have dissolved completely. If the solution appears cloudy, the dye has not fully dissolved.

In general, it's best to use dyes at room temperature, since any heat may affect the dyeing process. If you won't be using the solution right away, follow the directions given in the "Storage and Disposal" section of Chapter 2.

Note: Instructions for mixing fiber-reactive dye solutions using MX dyes are given in Chapter 9.

TIP

To make a mixing box for preparing dye solutions, turn a medium-sized box on its side and remove the lid. Line the box with newspaper or paper towels; spray them with water to dampen lightly. Do all your measuring and mixing inside the box, which serves as a hood, minimizing the chance of dye particles becoming airborne. The dampened paper absorbs any spilled powder.

DETERMINING DYE STOCK STRENGTH

The amount of dye powder dissolved in a certain volume of water determines the strength of a dye solution. Some dyers prefer to measure dye powders by volume using measuring spoons. This is fine for random dyeing methods or when reproducible results are not important.

Other dyers measure powder in grams using a scale, which is the most accurate way to measure consistently for repeatable results. Dye powders vary in density. Some are light and fluffy, some are dense and granular. The variation in texture makes it hard to use volume measurements for equal amounts of different colors.

I mix dye stock in two solution strengths - 1% and 0.1% - for all projects. Using the metric system makes this quite easy. To make a 1% solution I weigh 10 grams of dye and combine with 1000 ml of water. I create 0.1% dye stocks by measuring 1 gram of dye powder and mixing with 1000 ml of water, or by mixing 100 ml of a 1% solution with 900 ml of water (either way, the ratio of dye powder to volume of water is the same).

DETERMINING DEPTH OF SHADE

Depth of shade refers to the desired value (lightness or darkness) of the dyed fiber. It is expressed as a percentage indicating the weight of dye stuff (dye powder) in relation to the weight of dye goods (fiber). Using the metric system and 1% (or 0.1%) dye stocks makes it easy to calculate how much dye is needed to dye fiber to a particular depth of shade.

The formula for calculating how much dye stock to use is:

Weight of Dye Goods (fiber) × Depth of Shade ÷ Strength of Dye Stock = Amount of Dye Stock

To dye 1 pound of fiber (454 grams) to a 1% depth of shade using a 1% dye stock:

454 × 1 = 454
454 ÷ 1 = 454 ml of 1% dye stock

If you want a deeper color value (let's say a darker 2% depth of shade), change the numbers:

454 × 2 = 908 ml of 1% dye stock
908 ml ÷ 1 = 908 ml of 1% dye stock

For a pastel shade of the same color using a 1% dye stock:

454 × 0.1 = 45.4
45.4 ÷ 1 = 45.4 ml of 1% dye stock

Remember, you also use a weaker dye solution, a 0.1% dye stock, to obtain a paler value:

454 × 0.1 = 45.4
45.4 ÷ 0.1 = 454 ml of 0.1% dye stock

Primary colors are the foundation for a dyer's palette. Primary colors vary by type of dye and supplier. Alternative sets of mixing colors can be used in place of the basic red, yellow, and blue to extend the range of colors, since it's not possible to attain a full color spectrum with one set of primary dyes.

WashFast and Cushing Primary Colors

WASHFAST PRIMARY COLORS

WashFast dyes offer a range of *pure colors* (colors that are not composed of other colors in the dye powder) that can be used interchangeably for mixing a wide range of colors. The primaries that come closest to a "true" red, yellow, and blue are Bright Red 351, Sun Yellow 119, and Brilliant Blue 490.

WashFast Reds range from electric pinks (Magenta and Rhodamine Red) to more orange tones (Bright Red). The WashFast Reds are Magenta 338, Fuchsia 349, Bright Red 351, Red 366, and Rhodamine Red 370.

WashFast Yellows vary from having a slight green undertone (Flavine Yellow) to more of a gold undertone (Gold Yellow). The WashFast Yellows are Flavine Yellow 107A, Sun Yellow 119, Yellow 135, and Golden Yellow 199c.

WashFast dyes hold many options for blues, ranging from the basic blues—Brilliant Blue 490 or Bright Blue 440— or any of the hues in this extended blue family: Violet 817, National Blue 425c, Forest Green 725, Turquoise 478, Colonial Blue 401, or Navy 413.

CUSHING DYE PRIMARY COLORS

Cushing Perfection Dyes offer several possibilities for mixing primary colors. When creating my own colors with Cushing dyes, I use several different combinations of the following primary colors interchangeably. For reds, I use Turkey Red, Cherry, Aqualon Wine, or American Beauty. For yellows, I use either Canary or Yellow. Peacock and Blue are the mixing blues. The color wheel of skeins shown here uses American Beauty, Yellow, and Blue to form a soft color palette.

Ready-Made Colors

It takes time and practice working with primary colors to capture the exact shades. Dye companies offer a wide range of preformulated custom colors that take the guesswork out of mixing colors for an exact shade. This is a huge advantage if you don't have the time to experiment. Ready-made colors are proprietary blends of other dye colors in powder form. You can tell if a color is a blend by dampening a paper towel and gently tapping a tiny amount of dye powder from a spoon onto the damp paper. If a dye is made of component colors, you will see multicolored speckles on the paper. If a color is pure, the particles of dye on the filter paper will all be the same color. Be sure to wear a filter mask when doing this.

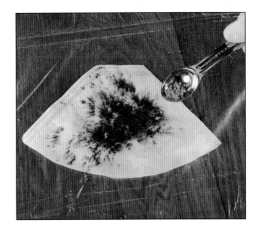

TIP

Working with Black

Adding black to primary hues creates shades that are more subdued. In general, you use black in the same strength stock solution as the color to which you are adding it. Achieving a solid black color requires mixing a very deep depth of shade.

CONTINUED ON NEXT PAGE

You can create exciting color recipes by working with blends of custom colors. Rug hookers are known for creating amazing palettes in rich, earthy hues. Since rug hookers dye in small quantities, the dye powder in their recipes is measured in very small amounts using grey dye spoons. Grey dye spoons are measuring spoons used to obtain accurate measurements of tiny amounts of dye powder. My set measures from $1/4$ teaspoon to $1/128$ teaspoon. Many rug-hooking dye recipe books are available, providing inspiration for any dyeing application.

My favorite recipe for a smoky tomato-red calls for $1/2$ teaspoon WashFast Bright Red 351, $1/4$ teaspoon WashFast Apricot 229, and $1/64$ teaspoon Colonial Blue 401. You can increase these proportions to produce a larger volume of dye stock.

There are a few disadvantages to working with custom colors. First, they tend to be more expensive than the primary colors. Second, there may be slight variations from batch to batch, which can be frustrating if you want highly repeatable results. Another drawback: If you want to have a wide selection of dyes on hand in your studio, you would need to stock many jars of custom dye colors. If you learn to mix your own colors using primary colors, you can have a broad palette by stocking just three to six primary colors.

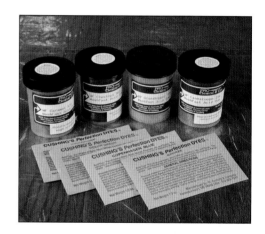

Creating a color wheel sampler is a good way to familiarize yourself with the basics of dyeing and blending primary hues. When you mix primaries, you quickly see how easy it is to create interesting and appealing colors. At the end of this exercise, you'll have sample skeins in a spectrum of color for future reference.

This project involves a series of mini-immersion dye baths. Each sample skein is dyed separately in its own 1-quart mason jar filled with dye stock and water.

Make Sampling Skeins

Fiber is a precious commodity. Sampling takes time but gives you a chance to test colors before dyeing large quantities only to discover that the result isn't what you wanted. Since it is difficult to judge colors from sample chips on paper, sample skeins more accurately portray how a color appears on fiber. Using sampling skeins that weigh at least 15 grams makes it easier to dye an accurate solid color sample. You will have enough yarn to try the test wrap process described later in this chapter.

1 Wind 12 sampling skeins of 25 yards each, using a worsted-weight wool yarn. Weigh the skeins individually and make a note of the result—mine weighed 15g each.

2 Loosely twist the skeins and place them in an acid presoak in a plastic bucket with a lid. The presoak should consist of 1 gallon warm water, 2 teaspoons Synthrapol, and 6 tablespoons citric acid crystals. Soak the skeins for 45 minutes prior to dyeing.

PRIMARY COLORS

Make a 1% dye stock solution for each of the WashFast primary colors (Sun Yellow 119, Bright Red 351, and Brilliant Blue 490) by following these steps:

Note: *First read the instructions and safety precautions for mixing dye stock on page 43.*

1 Measure 1g of dye powder using a digital scale and a weigh boat or plastic cup. Mix with 100ml of boiling water. Stir until all the dye powder is dissolved. Do the same to make 100ml dye stock for each primary color.

CONTINUED ON NEXT PAGE

2 Start by dyeing one skein using each of the primary colors. Determine how much dye solution to use for an immersion dye process by using the formula introduced earlier in the chapter. The dye stock strength is 1% and the desired depth of shade is also 1%. Multiply the weight of the fiber per dye pot (in this case, 1 skein = 15g) by the number of the depth of shade (DOS) then divide by the strength of the dye stock to calculate the amount of 1% dye solution needed.

Formula: WOF × DOS ÷ Dyestock Strength = # ml dye solution
Example: 15g × 1 ÷ 1 = 15ml dye solution (for each skein)

3 Determine the amount of water needed for the dye bath. Extra liquid is used in immersion dyeing so the dye can travel freely. In general, the ratio of water to weight of fiber is between 30:1 and 40:1. Since you are dyeing a very small amount of fiber, you can stick with the lower end of the ratio. A 30:1 ratio means you need 30ml liquid per each gram of fiber.

Ratio of Liquid Dye Bath to Fiber Weight
30:1
30ml × 15g fiber = 450ml total liquid in dye bath

4 Subtract the amount of liquid dye solution from the total amount of liquid needed for the dye bath. This tells you how much water you need.

Total amount of liquid needed for dye bath – Total amount of liquid dye stock = Amount of water to add
Example: 450ml of liquid needed – 15ml of dye stock = 435ml of water to add to each jar

5 Pour 15ml of dye solution and 435ml of room-temperature water into a measuring cup and stir to combine thoroughly. Place a skein of yarn in a mason jar and pour the liquid dye into the jar to cover the skein. Place the lid on the jar and shake to distribute the dye liquor evenly. Do this for each primary color.

SECONDARY COLORS

The next three skeins are the secondary colors.

1. Create each secondary color by mixing equal amounts of two primary colors. Since you need 15ml of dye stock for each skein, mix 7.5ml of two primary colors to make 15ml of a new secondary color. Use a 10ml syringe to measure small amounts of dye stock. Mix 15ml of three secondary colors using equal amounts (7.5ml) of primary dye stock.

2. Pour the dye stock plus 435ml water into a mason jar. Add a skein for each secondary color and shake to distribute the dye.

TERTIARY COLORS

Next, mix the dyes to form the tertiary colors. Tertiary colors fall between a primary and a secondary color on the color wheel. The tertiary colors for this project are a 75:25 blend of primary colors.

1. Tertiary color Red/Orange is 75% Red : 25% Yellow. To figure the amount of red dye liquid, multiply 15ml (the total amount needed to dye one skein) by 0.75 to get 11.25ml Red. To calculate the amount of Yellow, multiply 15 by 0.25 to get 3.75ml Yellow. This proportion of red to yellow creates the tertiary hue Red/Orange.

2. Mix the six tertiary hues as follows:

   Red/Orange: 75:25 11.25ml Red : 3.75ml Yellow
   Red/Purple: 75:25 11.25ml Red : 3.75ml Blue
   Blue/Purple: 75:25 11.25ml Blue : 3.75ml Red
   Blue/Green: 75:25 11.25ml Blue : 3.75ml Yellow
   Yellow/Green 75:25 11.25ml Yellow : 3.75ml Blue
   Yellow/Orange: 75:25 11.25ml Yellow: 3.75ml Red

Note: *It is hard to measure very small amounts of dye. For practical purposes you can round the above amounts to 11ml / 4ml.*

CONTINUED ON NEXT PAGE

3 Add 435ml water to each tertiary dye stock and mix well. Pour each solution into a mason jar containing a skein, place a lid on the jar, and shake.

4 To set the dye, steam the mason jars using an enamel canning pot with a jar rack and a lid. Add 2 inches of water to the bottom of the pot, place the jars on the rack, and bring the covered pot to a low boil. Maintain the simmer for 30 minutes. Allow the jars to cool before removing the skeins.

5 Rinse the skeins in warm water. Once they are dry, label each skein with the ratio of dye used to create the solution. You can place the skeins on a string to keep them together in the order of the color wheel.

Creating color wheels is a good way to become familiar with the range of primary colors. Repeat this exercise using alternate sets of primary colors to create a useful set of color reference samples.

Work with Color Concepts

The following exercises will help you become more familiar with the color concepts presented earlier in this chapter. The first pair of exercises illustrates two ways to alter a color's value: by varying the amount of dye or by adding black. The next demonstration shows how a color becomes less saturated by adding incremental amounts of its complement. The last exercise shows how to combine three primary colors for tertiary blends.

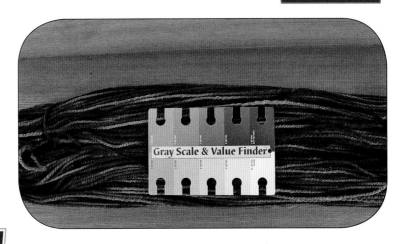

Understand the Concept of Values

VALUE CONTRAST EXERCISE

To create lighter values, add less dye to a stock solution. To create darker values, use more dye or add black dye solution in degrees to a dye stock.

This exercise works with painting a skein of yarn using dye stock in 3 strengths to see a range of value contrasts within one skein.

1 Mix a 1% dye solution of any acid dye hue (I used WashFast Plum).

2 Mix 10g dye powder with 1,000ml boiling water. Give the solution time to cool before proceeding to the next step.

You will now create two lighter values by decreasing the amount of dye powder.

3 Create a 0.5% stock solution by dissolving 5g dye powder in 1,000ml boiling water. Then make a 0.1% dye solution. The simplest way to do so is to pour 100ml of the 1% solution into a measuring cup and then add 900ml of water.

4 Wet out a 4-ounce skein of wool yarn using an acid presoak (see Chapter 4 for directions).

CONTINUED ON NEXT PAGE

5 Remove the skein from the acid presoak and press out the excess water. Lay the skein on a sheet of plastic wrap.

6 Use foam brushes to paint the skein in thirds. Begin with the weakest dye solution (the 0.1% shade).

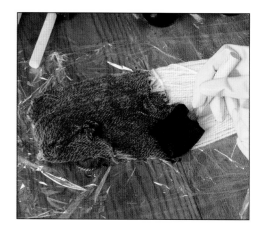

7 Apply the 0.5% dye to the middle section of the skein. Paint the remaining third of the skein using the 1% dye stock.

8 Flip the skein over to touch up any white spots, and blot to absorb any excess dye.

9 Wrap the skein in plastic and steam by placing the packet on a pie plate in a canning pot. Add 2 inches of water to the bottom, but do not let the water level reach the pie plate.

10 Steam the yarn for 45 minutes. Your finished skein will show a range of values for your chosen color.

TIP

Wrapping a skein in a plastic packet keeps all the color in contact with the fiber while the dye process takes place in steam. To make a plastic packet, start by folding in the ends of the plastic so they overlap the yarn or fiber. Fold the top edge of the plastic down over the fiber, then fold the bottom end up. Press to form a seal. Make a coil by loosely rolling the packet starting at one end. The photos on pages 107 and 108 show how to wrap fiber in plastic and how to roll the packet to place it in the steamer.

ADD BLACK TO CHANGE VALUE

Adding black to a color also alters its value. This exercise shows you how to use black to dampen a color. For this exercise, you need:

- 100ml of 1% dye stock in any color (I used WashFast Sun Yellow 119).
- 100ml of a 1% dye black stock (I used WashFast Black 672).
- White coffee filters cut into equal strips to create the color samples. Filter papers give an approximate representation of how the dye will appear on fiber and are helpful in gauging color.

① Set out 11 plastic cups. Use a plastic 10ml syringe to measure the dyes in the following proportions:

Cup 1: 10ml black
Cup 2: 9ml black, 1ml yellow
Cup 3: 8ml black, 2ml yellow
Cup 4: 7ml black, 3ml yellow
Cup 5: 6ml black, 4ml yellow
Cup 6: 5ml black, 5ml yellow
Cup 7: 4ml black, 6ml yellow
Cup 8: 3ml black, 7ml yellow
Cup 9: 2ml black, 8ml yellow
Cup 10: 1ml black, 9ml yellow
Cup 11: 10ml yellow

② Stir each cup to blend the dyes. Dip a coffee filter paper into each cup to absorb the dye completely.

③ Set the filter papers on the table in sequence to dry and then compare them to see the progression of values made by adding black to a color. Compare your results using a grayscale tool.

CONTINUED ON NEXT PAGE

Change Color Saturation with Complements

Bright colors are highly saturated in color. Adding amounts of a pure hue's complement (see "The Color Wheel" earlier in this chapter) subdues the color. It also changes its value. To see how adding a complement changes saturation, you can duplicate the exercise on the previous page. Use the color wheel to select a color and its complement and create 100ml of 1% dye stock for each of the two colors. In the example, I use WashFast Sun Yellow 119 and Violet 817. *(Illustration courtesy of the Color Wheel Company.)*

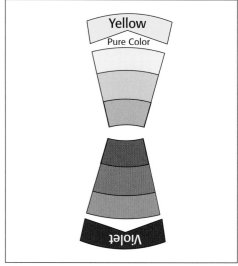

① Set up 11 plastic cups. Measure the dyes into each cup in the following proportions using a 10ml plastic syringe:

Cup 1: 10ml violet
Cup 2: 9ml violet, 1ml yellow
Cup 3: 8ml violet, 2ml yellow
Cup 4: 7ml violet, 3ml yellow
Cup 5: 6ml violet, 4ml yellow
Cup 6: 5ml violet, 5ml yellow
Cup 7: 4ml violet, 6ml yellow
Cup 8: 3ml violet, 7ml yellow
Cup 9: 2ml violet, 8ml yellow
Cup 10: 1ml violet, 9ml yellow
Cup 11: 10ml yellow

② Dip a strip of filter paper into each cup.

③ When the papers have dried, label the proportions of **color : complement** for future reference.

Compare the results of this exercise with the results of the previous exercise. The color Sun Yellow was changed by adding black and then by adding its complement, Violet. The addition of black deadens a color while toning it down; the addition of a complement tones down the original color but gives a richer, more interesting result.

Create Tertiary Color Combinations

Colors made by blending three primaries in varying proportions create a unified palette, since all colors are present in each new color. A color made by blending three primaries is a tertiary color. This fun, hand-painted yarn exercise shows how you can create many different color combinations by mixing three primary colors in varying proportions. It will help you become more skilled in the very satisfying process of creating your own colors. You can repeat this exercise using any combination of primary colors.

MATERIALS

- 4 four-ounce wool skeins, presoaked in acid solution (see Chapter 4)
- 1,000ml 0.1% dye stock, WashFast primary colors Sun Yellow 119, Red 351, and Navy 413
- Foam brushes
- Plastic wrap
- Canning pot with lid and pie plate for steaming skeins

SKEIN A

For the first skein, mix the primary colors in the following proportions to create three new colors:

> Tertiary Blend #1: Yellow 80ml, Red 10ml, Navy 10ml
> Tertiary Blend #2: Yellow 70ml, Red 20ml, Navy 10ml
> Tertiary Blend #3: Yellow 60ml, Red 20ml, Navy 20ml

Lay the skein on a sheet of plastic wrap. Use foam brushes to apply the colors to the yarn in bands of equal length, approximately 4 inches. Wrap the skein in plastic and set aside.

SKEIN B

Paint the next skein using blends of the same colors in different proportions, with red being the dominant hue. Mix three new colors as follows:

> Tertiary Blend #1: Yellow 30ml, Red 60ml, Navy 10ml
> Tertiary Blend #2: Yellow 30ml, Red 50ml, Navy 20ml
> Tertiary Blend #3: Yellow 30ml, Red 40ml, Navy 30ml

Lay a skein on the table and apply 4 inch swatches of each color sequence as you did with the first skein. Wrap the skein in plastic and set it aside.

CONTINUED ON NEXT PAGE

SKEIN C

Mix the dyes in the following proportions and paint another skein:

Yellow 50ml, Red 40ml, Navy 10ml
Yellow 40ml, Red 50ml, Navy 10ml
Yellow 40ml, Red 10ml, Navy 50ml

SKEIN D

Paint the last skein following these proportions:

Yellow 80 ml, Red 10ml, Navy 10ml
Yellow 40 ml, Red 50ml, Navy 10ml
Yellow 40 ml, Red 10ml, Navy 50ml

Paint the last skein and wrap it in plastic. Set all four plastic-wrapped skeins in the canning pot to steam for 45 minutes. When they are cool, rinse and hang the skeins to dry.

Compare the skeins. Yellow is the predominant color in skein A, with red and navy used in nearly equal portions. The overall colors are orange and gold, and the color shifts are subtle. In skein B, red is the dominant color. The colors transition from orange-red to rose-red to a soft purple-red. Again, the changes in color are subtle.

In skein C, there is more color contrast and a greater range in values due to the higher percentage of navy in one of the tertiary blends. The color proportions in skein D also create higher contrast within the skein. The colors range from gold and orange-red to a warm reddish brown.

It's exciting to discover new colors by varying the proportions of the three primaries. You can further explore the possibilities of tertiary blends by using different primary colors. Label your samples and keep records of the colors and proportions used.

It is helpful to use a color wheel when planning color palettes for dye projects. A *color palette* is a color scheme for a particular dye project. The basic color schemes are monochromatic, complementary, analogous, split complementary, and triadic. Use any of these schemes to design color palettes. The back side of this color wheel tool clearly illustrates these color relationships. *(Photo courtesy of the Color Wheel Company.)*

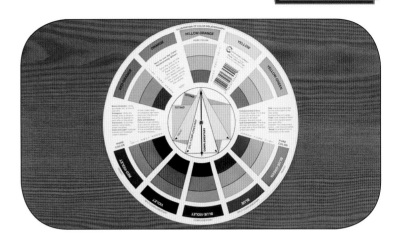

Types of Color Schemes

MONOCHROMATIC COLOR SCHEMES

Monochromatic schemes are visually pleasing and the easiest to understand. When you look at any slice of the color wheel, you see a hue family with the shades and tints of that color family. The skeins in the photo show a monochromatic color sequence.

COMPLEMENTARY COLOR SCHEMES

Pairing *complementary* colors creates dynamic contrasts because the colors are in opposition on the color wheel. Placing a color beside its complement makes both colors vibrate because of the high contrast of hue. The yarn sample on the right shows how equal portions of the complementary colors red and green were plied together for a lively effect. Small amounts of complementary colors viewed at a distance appear to cancel each other out. The eye mixes the two and sees a muddy blend, rather than two distinct, vibrant colors. This is called *optical mixing.* The left yarn sample shows a blending of complements to produce a muted color, where nearly equal amounts of red and green were carded together before spinning.

CONTINUED ON NEXT PAGE

ANALOGOUS COLOR SCHEMES

Analogous color plans are composed of adjacent colors on a color wheel. The hue progression is subtle and creates a harmonious blend (rather than the high hue contrast of complements). Generally, analogous color plans stay within quadrants of the color wheel: blue-green-yellow, yellow-orange-red, red-purple-blue. For new dyers, analogous color plans are a safe place to start.

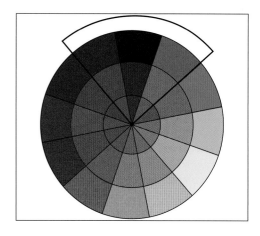

SPLIT COMPLEMENTARY COLOR SCHEMES

In a *split complementary* color relationship, you select a key color, find its complement, and then identify the colors on either side of its complement. For example, if the key color is violet, its complement is yellow. The split complements for violet are the colors on either side of yellow: yellow-green and yellow-orange. This hue combination is not quite as intense as direct complements and provides a wider palette range. When using a split complementary color palette, try giving more weight to the key color, using the split complements as accents or giving more weight to the closely related split complements (in this case yellow green and yellow orange) and using the complement (violet) as an accent.

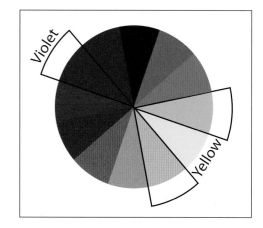

TRIADIC COLOR SCHEMES

Triadic colors are three colors that are equally spaced apart from one another on a color wheel. The primary colors red, yellow, and blue form a triad. On a 12-color color wheel, triads are three spaces apart from one another. Violet, orange, and green are another example of a triad. Experiment with proportion when using a triadic color composition for dyeing fibers.

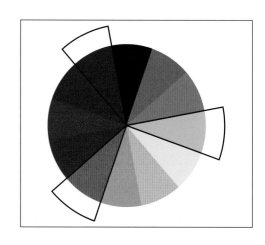

Work with Color Proportions and Progressions

USE FILTER PAPERS

Understanding how to use color proportions is a bit like understanding how to find the right balance of spices in cooking. Sampling is a good way to get a sense of how much of each color creates a pleasing result. I use several methods to decide for choosing the right balance and the most pleasing progression of colors for a palette. Painting dye colors directly on coffee filter papers is a good way to test color proportions before dyeing yarn or roving. Apply colors to several papers, then fold the papers or arrange them in different sequences to see which color progression works best.

DYE YARN SAMPLES

Another way to experiment with color is to dye sample yarn skeins in the colors you're considering for your project using the Mason jar immersion method described earlier in this chapter. After you have dyed your samples, wrap the yarn around a 5-x-7-inch index card in varying color progressions. Try placing different colors adjacent to each other and experiment with color proportions. Use this information to determine color order and length of repeats in hand-painted yarns.

USE THE FIBONACCI SERIES

Artists use *Fibonacci numbers* to arrive at pleasing color proportions. (They are also called the "golden ratio" for that reason.) The proportions created from a sequence of Fibonacci numbers are found in nature as well as in art. A Fibonacci number sequence starts with 1 and progresses like this: 1, 1, 2, 3, 5, 8, 13, 21, . . . with the next number in the series always being the sum of the two preceding numbers.

The sequence can be used in several ways. You can use it to determine color proportions in a multicolored carded batt. For example, measure three colors in these amounts: 3, 5, 8 ounces; then card them together in three stripes. Use the same number sequence to paint a skein of yarn or a hank of roving. The lower end of the sequence from 3 to 13 is more effective.

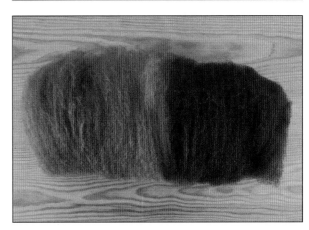

Other Color Considerations

WORK WITH COLOR TEMPERATURE

Consider color temperature when planning a palette. Warm hues—reds, oranges, and yellows—stand out. Cool colors—blues, greens, and violets—recede.

Using a dash of a warm color in a predominantly cool composition adds a spark of excitement. Cool colors will tone down a warm color palette.

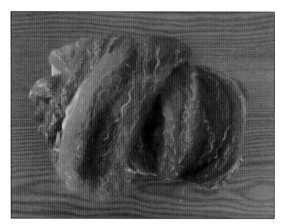

Warm colors.   *Cool colors.*

DEVELOPING COLOR INTUITION

The more you experiment with color in dyeing, the more confident you will become. When learning to create color schemes, start by working within your color comfort zone, selecting three or four analogous hues for painting yarn skeins or roving. Then choose one of your colors as a key color and find its complements and split complements. Use those schemes to create a series of painted skeins or roving.

To gain more confidence in creating tertiary blends, select any three primary colors and begin blending. You can try using the proportions in the exercise on pages 57 and 58, or you can simply work by eye, adding small amounts of one color to another until you create an appealing new color. If you measure the added amounts of dye, you will be able to repeat your results.

To become more comfortable in a more freehand way, try a series of direct-pour dye baths using the low-water method described in Chapter 8. Mix dyes in colors you love, but limit yourself to three at a time when you pour them on the fiber. Try different combinations. It's exciting to see new colors form as dyes merge in the pot.

As you become more comfortable with dye procedures and more familiar with how colors interact, you can step back from the structured approaches described in this chapter. That's when dyeing really becomes exciting. You will learn from each experiment. Keep track of your results and how you arrived at them.

The colors found in nature provide an unending source of inspiration for color work in the dye studio. Whether it be the exuberant colors of a sunrise or the lichen growing on the side of a tree, train your eye to notice nature's palette. A camera is a helpful tool for capturing images to analyze color compositions more closely.

Sometimes inspiration is found in the big picture. The colors of a sunrise were the inspiration for the colors that became a series of drum-carded batts of wool and silk.

CONTINUED ON NEXT PAGE

A drive down a country road can also inspire a palette. Autumn ferns by the roadside appear as a mosaic of greens, pale yellows, golds, and rusts. To capture these colors in hand-painted skeins, I used a two-step process of applying a soft background color (pale gold) and layering shades of greens and golds using a technique I call Atmospheric Effects (see Chapter 10).

Sometimes examining nature up close reveals a palette. A cluster of berries on a bittersweet vine inspired the colors in this brushed mohair yarn dyed using a resist technique. The process of dyeing using a resist is described in Chapter 10.

Keep a Color Journal and Work Records

Create a color journal as a catalog of colors and palettes that draw your eye. Clip images from calendars, magazines, advertisements, and catalogs. Include textile swatches or scraps of commercial yarn. A scrapbook is perfect for assembling your collection of images.

Sort through the images you have gathered and group the images by color themes. Everyone has color preferences, so don't be surprised to see that your images may be heavily weighted toward your favorite hues. If you are attracted to a smaller part of a larger image, cut out the colors that appeal to you. The idea is to collect colors, not pictures.

Study the groups of images more closely. See if you can make further groupings based on dominant hues, warm or cool colors, high or low values, and analogous hues or strong hue contrasts. Use a glue stick to arrange the images on the pages of a scrapbook and use them to inspire future projects.

Keeping records of your work in the dye studio is crucial if you wish to repeat your results in the future. Essential information to record includes the following:

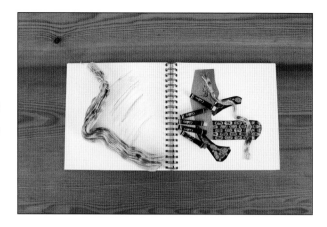

- Manufacturer and type of dye
- Name and number of the color
- Date
- Stock solution (number of teaspoons/grams of dye powder per cup [250ml] of water)
- Type of fiber and the form (for example: silk/yarn; wool/roving)
- Amount of fiber in ounces/grams
- Amount of dye to weight of goods/fiber
- Amount of leveling agent per pot
- Type and amount of assist per pot (acid, soda ash)
- Details about the process and method of application

You should also keep a swatch of yarn or fiber as a color sample of each dye batch. You can attach the swatch to your sample sheet. If you make test skeins, attach labels directly to the skeins.

Immersion Dye Project Record

Date: _____

Type of Fiber / Preparation: _____ Source: _____

Type of Dye: _____

Colors / % Dye stock: _____

Amount of fiber / pot: _____

Amount of dye / pot: _____

Glauber Salt: _____ Synthrapol: _____

Volume of water / dye assists / pot:

Citric Acid Crystals: _____ White Vinegar: _____

Soda Ash: _____ Other: _____

Cook time / method: _____

Notes: _____

_____

Hand Paint Dye Project Record

Date: _____

Type of Fiber / Preparation: _____ Source: _____

Weight of Fiber: _____

Presoak: _____

Type of Dye: _____

Colors, % Dye Stock: _____

Application
Method: _____

Color / Volume Dye Solution per container:

Container 1: _____ Container 2: _____

Container 3: _____ Container 4: _____

Container 5: _____ Container 6: _____

Additional materials used (amount per container):

Citric Acid Crystals: _____ White Vinegar: _____

Thickener (type): _____ Urea: _____

Notes: _____

6

Immersion Dyeing: Wool and Protein Fibers

Immersion dyeing is the process of creating a dye bath in large pot, adding fiber, and heating it over a period of time. The "bath" contains water, dye, acid (either citric acid crystals or white vinegar), Glauber salt (usually), and Synthrapol. Heating the dye bath triggers the chemical bond between fiber and dye. Because large pots are used, this process is sometimes called *kettle-dyeing*.

Immersion dyeing is traditionally used to dye solid colors. Hand-dyed solids have rich tonal characteristics and subtle variations of shade that set them apart from commercially dyed solid colors. This method can also be used for semisolid and rainbow dyeing yarn, roving, wool locks, and fabric.

Successful immersion dye baths rely in part on using stock pots (either stainless steel or unchipped enamel) large enough to accommodate the weight of fiber. Dye pots of adequate size ensure even temperature and dye distribution. In general a 20-quart pot will comfortably dye 8 ounces (227g) of fiber. A 40-quart for will handle 1 pound (454g) of fiber without crowding. Wider pots work better than deeper pots. They allow the fiber to float horizontally, avoiding contact with the bottom of the pot.

Note: *Make sure the size of your burner and dye pot are compatible to avoid the danger of a tipping dye pot.*

Long-handled spoons, tongs, or dowels are useful for manipulating the fiber in the dye bath.

Prepare your dye solutions in advance, following the instructions in Chapter 5. Unless otherwise noted, dye solutions work best when used at room temperature. The guidelines given in Chapter 4 show how to prepare yarn and fiber for immersion dyeing.

When immersion dyeing, you will be working over a simmering pot of hot water. Use an exhaust fan and wear a dual cartridge respirator mask to avoid inhaling the vapors from the dye pot. Safety glasses will protect your eyes from splashes. Wear insulated gloves to protect your hands from steam and hot water. Please review the safety guidelines in Chapter 2 before starting any dye project, and always follow the product manufacturer's usage guidelines.

Note: *See Chapter 2 for instructions on disposing of exhausted dye baths and for ways to use unexhausted dye baths and leftover dye.*

Many factors come into play in the process of hand-dyeing solid-shade yarn. You must use a pot large enough to allow for sufficient circulation of the *dye liquor* (the liquid of the dye bath) and even temperature distribution. Careful measuring of materials, continuous monitoring of temperature, and manipulating the fibers in the dye bath throughout the process contribute to reaching an even shade.

This section describes how to dye 1 pound (454g) of wool yarn using WashFast acid dye.

MATERIALS

- 4 four-ounce skeins (454g) of wool yarn prepared for dyeing (see Chapter 4)
- WashFast dye Teal 495, 2 cups (500ml) of a 1% solution (see instructions in Chapter 5)
- 1 tablespoon (15g) Glauber salt
- 1 teaspoon (5ml) Synthrapol
- 1 tablespoon (15g) citric acid crystals or 11 tablespoons (165ml) white vinegar

TOOLS

- 40-quart stainless steel or enamel stock pot
- Long-handled spoon or wooden dowel
- Thermometer

PREPARE THE SKEINS

1. See "Wind and Tie Yarn Skeins" in Chapter 4. You will need at least three figure-8 ties to keep the skeins from tangling. Looping a shoestring leash through the skeins makes handling them easier.

2. Soak the skeins for 30 minutes in a sink or basin filled with warm water and ½ teaspoon Synthrapol (see "Wet Out the Fiber" in Chapter 4). This removes any dirt or spinning oil used in the yarn's processing and opens up the fibers so that the wool will more easily accept the dye molecules.

CONTINUED ON NEXT PAGE

The Dye Bath

MIX THE DYE STOCK

Create 2 cups / 500ml of a 1% dye stock by mixing 5 grams of dye powder with 500ml of boiling water. See Chapter 5 for complete instructions and safety measures for mixing dye stock.

HOW MUCH DYE STOCK?

In general, 500ml of a 1% dye stock is enough to dye one pound of fiber a deep color.

If you need consistent, repeatable results use the metric system and the formula presented in Chapter 5 for percentage dyeing:

Weight of Dye Goods × Depth of Shade ÷ Strength of Dye Stock = Amount of Dye Stock Needed

Here is the formula for dyeing one pound / 454g of yarn to a 1% depth of shade using a 1% dye stock:

454g × 1 (DOS) = 454

454 ÷ 1 (Strength of Dye Stock) = 454ml of 1% dye stock

HOW MUCH LIQUID?

As a rule of thumb, 3½ gallons is a sufficient amount of water for dyeing one pound/454g of fiber.

As explained in Chapter 5, the ratio of liquid (which includes dye stock and water) to fiber is approximately 30:1.

If using percentage dyeing for repeatable results, you would use a formula to calculate the volume of liquid using the metric system. Multiply the weight of dye goods times 30 to arrive at the total volume of liquid needed.

454g × 30 = 13,620ml Total Amount Dye Liquor Needed

Remember to subtract the volume of dye stock (in this case 454ml) from the total to calculate the amount of water to add to the dye bath:

13, 620ml – 454 = 13,166ml (or 13.2 liters) total amount of water

Note: 13.2 liters is very close to the ball-park volume of 3 ½ gallons liquid per pound of fiber.

PREPARE THE BATH

1 Fill a 40-quart stainless steel stock pot (or an unchipped enamel pot of similar size) with 3½ gallons room-temperature water. Add 1 teaspoon Synthrapol to the pot and stir.

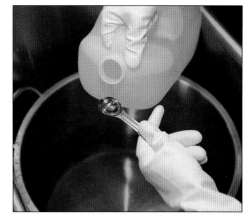

2 Predissolve 1 tablespoon Glauber salt in ½ cup warm water, and then add it to the pot. The salt tends to crystallize in water, so make sure it has fully dissolved.

Glauber salt serves as a *leveling agent*. It forms a temporary bond with the fiber, slowing and inhibiting the process of the dye molecules bonding with the fiber. This enables the dye to bond more evenly and helps achieve color uniformity. In general, 1 tablespoon of Glauber salt for each pound (454g) of fiber in the dye bath is sufficient.

3 Add 1 tablespoon citric acid crystals to the pot. Stir well so that the crystals dissolve completely.

Citric acid acts as a *dye assist*. It alters the pH of the dye bath (acid dyes work in the pH range of 4–6) and, along with heat, causes the dye molecules to bond with the fibers. White vinegar can be substituted for citric acid crystals. You typically use 1 tablespoon of citric acid crystals (or 11 tablespoons of white vinegar) per pound (454g) of fiber in the dye bath.

4 Add the dissolved dye solution to the pot and stir well.

CONTINUED ON NEXT PAGE

Dye the Skeins

1 Remove the skeins from the presoak and gently squeeze the excess water from the yarn. Use your washing machine to spin out the excess water, which can slow the uptake of dye.

2 Wearing insulated rubber gloves, add the skeins to the dye bath. Lift and submerge the skeins several times to saturate them evenly. Make sure the dye is able to penetrate beneath the figure-8 ties. Give the bath a stir each time you lift the skeins.

3 Place the pot on your cooking surface with the heat set to medium-high.

> **Note:** Be sure to ventilate the dyeing area and take care when stirring the dye bath and handling the hot fiber. Wear your respirator mask, safety glasses, and insulated gloves when working near the dye pot.

4 The temperature of the dye bath will rise gradually at first. Use a thermometer to monitor the temperature continually. Keep in mind that the water at the bottom of the pot will heat more quickly than the water at the top of the pot. Lift the skeins and stir continuously. This is essential for an even dye strike.

TIP

Do not allow the skeins to sit at the bottom of the pot. This may create dark spots of color on the yarn.

5 Continue to monitor the temperature, lifting the skeins and stirring the dye bath periodically. The temperature of the dye bath will climb more quickly once it reaches 140°F (60°C). 160°F (71°C) is the magic threshold where you will see that most of the dye has fixed on the fiber and very little is left in the water. You should notice the yarn deepening in color as the dye bonds with the fiber. As this happens, the dye bath becomes more clear.

6 For dyeing wool, WashFast dyes need to simmer just beneath a low boil [212°F (100°C)] for at least 45 minutes. This is necessary to achieve a light-fast and washfast bond.

Note: If there is quite a bit of color remaining in the pot after 60 minutes, lift the skeins from the bath, add 6 tablespoons of white vinegar, and stir. Replace the skeins and simmer for an additional 10 minutes to exhaust the dye bath.

Rinse the Skeins

1 Turn off the heat and allow the pot to sit until the water reaches room temperature. The water in the dye pot should be clear, indicating that the dye bath is *exhausted*. A dye bath has exhausted when all the dye molecules have bonded with the fiber and the water is clear.

2 If, at the end of the cooking time, there is still dye left in the bath, allow the dye bath to cool completely. Often any residual dye will still bond with the fiber. When the dye bath has exhausted, the water will be completely clear.

3 Fill a sink or washbasin with warm water and ½ teaspoon Synthrapol. Submerge the skeins in the soak. This after-bath will remove any excess dye that has not bonded with the yarn.

4 Make a second rinse with cool water and submerge the skeins.

5 Press or spin out any excess water and hang the skeins to dry.

6 See Chapter 4 for instructions for using unexhausted dye baths and for dye bath disposal.

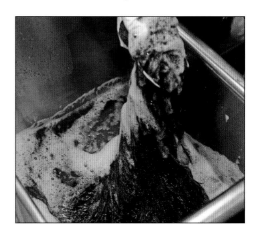

It's possible to achieve a mottled effect in an immersion dye bath by tweaking the instructions for a solid-shade dyeing. Semisolid yarns have subtle color variations. Visually, the colors are not quite solid but not quite variegated. The results are achieved using a WashFast dye formed of composite colors (see Chapter 5). Manipulating the temperature encourages the dye to break into its component colors for a marbled effect.

MATERIALS

- 4 four-ounce (454g) wool yarn skeins, prepared for dyeing (see Chapter 4)
- 1¾ teaspoon (4.5g) WashFast dye Herb Green 709
- 1 teaspoon (5ml) Synthrapol
- 1 tablespoon (15g) citric acid crystals or 11 tablespoons (165ml) white vinegar
- 40-quart stainless steel or enamel pot
- Long-handled spoon or wooden dowel

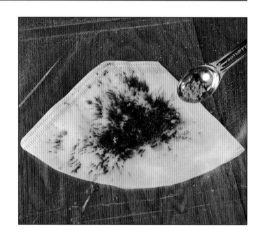

PREPARE THE DYE SOLUTION

For this process, the dye solution must be hot when added to the bath. Do not mix the solution until you're ready to run the dye bath. Follow the safety guidelines for mixing dye solutions in Chapter 5.

1 Add the dye powder to a glass measuring cup. Mix with 2 tablespoons boiling water to form a paste. Then add boiling water to make 2 cups of dye solution.

2 Stir thoroughly to dissolve all dye powder and set aside.

SET UP THE DYE BATH

1 The trick to this process is adding the fiber to a hot dye bath which causes some of the color to strike quickly. Fill the stock pot with 3½ gallons hot water [110°F (43°C)]. Add the Synthrapol and stir to combine.

2 Add the citric acid crystals and stir thoroughly.

3 Pour the hot dye solution into the pot and stir.

ADD THE SKEINS TO THE DYE BATH

1 Add the skeins to the dye bath. Lift and submerge the skeins several times allowing the dye to penetrate all strands. Make sure the dye travels beneath the yarn ties. The fiber will grab the dye color very quickly because the dye pot is hot and acid is present.

2 Place the dye pot on a heat source set to medium-high. Every 5 minutes, lift the skeins with a slotted spoon and stir the dye pot. The dye will strike the skeins somewhat unevenly. In some places the skeins will appear blue. In other places, the fiber will appear more green or yellow. The uneven distribution of temperature causes more variation in the dye strike because different colors strike at different temperatures. Blues strike at lower temperatures, whereas greens and yellows strike at a higher temperature.

3 When dyeing for an uneven effect, I stir the pot less frequently as the temperature rises. Monitor the pot and turn the skeins with a slotted spoon approximately every 5 minutes for the first 15 minutes. Keep the water just beneath the boiling point and maintain that temperature for at least 45 minutes. The dye bath should appear clear at that time. Allow the skeins to cool completely.

4 Rinse the skeins following the same instructions for rinsing skeins in a solid-shade dye bath. Hang the yarn out of direct sunlight to dry.

Immersion dye baths create vibrant solid or multicolored roving. This section describes how to create a variegated roving from an immersion dye process.

Be careful when handling roving during the dye process in order to avoid felting. Felting occurs when the scales on the surface of the wool fibers become locked together during the dye process due to heat and agitation. Once fiber becomes felted, it is useless for handspinning.

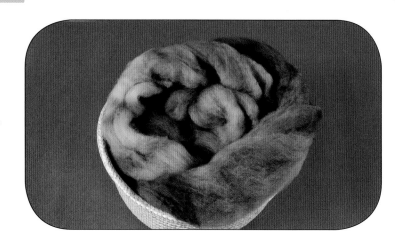

MATERIALS

- 2 eight-ounce (227g) hanks of wool roving, prepared for dyeing (see Chapter 4)
- WashFast dyes, 2 cups (500ml) of 1% solution of each color: Grasshopper 719, Turquoise 478, and Teal 495

- 2 tablespoons citric acid crystals
- 2 twenty-quart stock pots
- Long-handled spoon

Roving Preparation

PREPARE THE DRY ROVING

1. Weigh out 1 pound of wool roving and divide it into two 8-ounce sections. When immersion-dyeing roving, it's very important not to crowd the dye pot—this will lead to felting! Dye each piece of roving in its own pot.

2. Form a bundle of roving by laying the fiber out on a table in a zigzag fashion. Loosely tie the bundle in two places with string or a shoelace to make the roving easier to handle.

WETTING OUT THE FIBER

1 Fill a sink or basin with warm water to which you have added ½ teaspoon Synthrapol.

2 Gently press the roving into the water, making sure that all air bubbles escape from the fiber. Do not swish or agitate the fiber. Allow the roving to soak for at least 1 hour.

PREPARE THE DYE AND DYE BATH

1 Prepare dye solutions for each of the three colors, each in its own measuring cup, following the instructions in Chapter 5.

2 Fill each pot with 3 gallons room-temperature water. Add ½ teaspoon Synthrapol to each pot and stir. Add 1 tablespoon citric acid crystals to each pot and stir.

3 Add 1 cup (250ml) of the Grasshopper dye solution to each pot and stir.

CONTINUED ON NEXT PAGE

Dye the Roving

ADD ROVING TO DYE POTS

1 Remove the bundles of roving from the presoak and gently squeeze out the excess water. Remove the ties from the bundles before adding the fiber to the dye pots. Try to maintain the zigzag arrangement. Press gently to submerge the fiber, but do not agitate the wool.

2 Place the dye pots on the heat source. Gradually raise the temperature. To ensure that the dye is distributed evenly throughout the dye pot, lift the fiber carefully with one slotted spoon while gently stirring the pot with another spoon.

3 Allow the dye bath to reach a low simmer, but do not allow it to boil. Monitor the temperature carefully. When the thermometer reaches 160°F (71°C), the first color will have nearly exhausted.

4 Add 1 teaspoon citric acid crystals to the Teal and Turquoise dye solutions. Stir thoroughly.

TIP

Adding acid directly to the dye solutions will cause the dye to bond more quickly upon striking the fiber. This gives you more control when directly applying color to a dye bath.

Dye the Roving

1 Once the Grasshopper base color has bonded with the roving, directly apply a ribbon of Turquoise by carefully pouring approximately 50ml from the measuring cup. Allow the dye to absorb where it strikes the roving.

2 Each color will strike quickly as it comes into contact with the roving. Do not stir the bath or manipulate the fiber. This will spread the dye, and you don't want to change the overall color of the roving. Allowing the color to sit where it lands contributes to the variegated effect.

3 Once the Turquoise dye has been absorbed, apply the Teal dye in a ribbon in the same manner. Allow the roving to absorb the dye.

4 You may gently press down on (but do not stir) the fiber so that any loose dye will disperse and bond with the roving. Allow the pot to simmer (but not boil) for 45 minutes, giving the dyes time to bond with the fiber.

TIP

When adding dyes to a multicolor dye bath, always start with the lightest colors and then add the darker shades. Be careful not to overwhelm the paler colors by adding too much of a darker color.

CONTINUED ON NEXT PAGE

Rinse the Fiber

1 Once the fiber has cooled completely, carefully remove it from the dye bath using both hands to support its weight.

2 Fill a sink with tepid water and submerge the roving to rinse away any residual dye. Do not agitate the fiber.

3 Lift the fiber from the soak and gently press to remove excess water. Lay the roving on a table or drying rack, and allow the excess water to drip off.

4 When the roving is fully dry, it may look compressed. You can carefully ease the fibers apart if they feel sealed together. Take care not to break the roving while drafting.

Immersion dye baths can create vividly dyed wool locks in multiple colors—all in one pot.

This section uses PRO One Shot dyes to dye 1 pound of wool locks. One Shot dyes contain everything you need; it's not necessary to add acid or salt in the dyeing process.

MATERIALS

- 1 pound (454g) wool locks (see Chapter 4 for preparation guidelines)
- PRO One Shot dyes, 3 teaspoons (7.5g) of each color: OS37 Persimmon, OS30 Rust, and OS26 Autumn
- ½ teaspoon (2.5ml) Synthrapol

- 20-quart stainless steel or enamel stock pot
- 2 net laundry bags
- Long-handled spoon

PREPARE THE FIBER AND DYES

1 Scour the wool ahead of time following the instructions in Chapter 4. Removing dirt and lanolin will make it easier for the fiber to accept dye. Divide the wool and place 8 ounces (227g) of locks in each of two net laundry bags for the presoak.

2 Fill a sink with warm water [110°F (44°C)] and ½ teaspoon Synthrapol. Submerge the bags in the sink and allow the wool to soak for 30 minutes.

CONTINUED ON NEXT PAGE

3 Create the dye solution by mixing 3 teaspoons of each One Shot color with 1 cup (250ml) boiling water. See Chapter 5 for instructions and safety guidelines for mixing dye solutions. Stir the solution until completely dissolved.

PREPARE THE DYE BATH

1 Add 3 gallons room-temperature water to the dye pot and place the pot on the cooking surface over medium-high heat.

2 Remove the wetted-out fiber from the laundry bags and place it in the dye pot. Distribute the fiber evenly inside the pot.

ADD COLORS TO THE DYE BATH

1 Beginning with Autumn, the lightest shade, pour the dye solution over one third area of the dye pot. Do not stir.

TIP

Take care when handling wool locks in the dyeing process. If you agitate or stir the fibers too vigorously, they will felt together and you will have a useless tangled mass.

2 Add the second color, Rust, to one third of the dye pot. Try to avoid overlapping colors.

3 Add the last color, Persimmon, to the remaining third of the dye pot. Give the wool a few minutes to absorb each color. Do not stir the pot.

4 Gently tap the side of the pot with a spoon. This will encourage the dyes to migrate slightly but will not cause the three colors to completely blend.

5 Allow the pot to reach a boil and gently simmer for 30 minutes.

6 When the dye bath has cooled completely, transfer the locks back into the net bags. Rinse the wool fibers in a sink full of tepid water. Spread the locks on a table or rack to dry.

TIP

To speed the drying time, use a salad spinner to remove excess water from the locks.

Dyeing silk scarves is a fun way to use leftover dyes. It's also a neat way to experiment with mixing colors and to explore textile surface design techniques. Keep a stash of silk scarf blanks (available from dye supply companies, listed in the appendix) on hand to absorb the color left over in unexhausted dye baths.

The two-part process described here uses silk blanks in a technique that involves immersion dyeing (in two steps) and a shibori resist technique to create pattern. *Shibori* is a Japanese technique for wrapping fibers to create areas that resist dyes. You can create exciting color patterns by experimenting with resists and dyes.

MATERIALS

- Four 11-×-60-inch crepe de chine silk scarf blanks
- An unexhausted acid dye bath
- Leftover acid dyes

The remaining tools depend on which resist method you use:

- Iron
- White cotton string
- Embroidery or small scissors
- Glass marbles
- Needle and thread
- Mason jars

Dye the Scarves (Step 1)

1 Place the blank scarves in a warm presoak with ½ teaspoon Synthrapol. Allow them to soak for at least 1 hour.

2 An unexhausted dye bath with a visible amount of leftover dye will dye the scarves a pale overall color. You may add more dye to the unexhausted bath to deepen the color. Add more dye in small increments (25ml at a time). Check the dye bath, making sure the pH range is between 4 and 6. Add 1 teaspoon citric acid crystals if needed.

3 Add the scarves to the dye bath and gradually raise the temperature of the bath to 185°F (85°C). Do not let the temperature go beyond this point or it will ruin the luster of the silk. Allow the scarves to simmer for 30 minutes.

4 When the dye bath has cooled completely, rinse the scarves in warm water. Then hang them on a rack to dry.

CONTINUED ON NEXT PAGE

Create the Resist and Dye (Steps 2 and 3)

There are several methods for creating designs on fabric using resists. Each method creates a different pattern. After you wrap, fold, or tie the scarf, you overdye it in a contrasting color. When the dye is set and the scarf is dry, remove the resist and admire the pattern you have created.

STITCH, GATHER, AND DYE

1 Use a fine sewing needle and thread to make ¼-inch stitches about 1 inch apart at intervals across the width of the scarf.

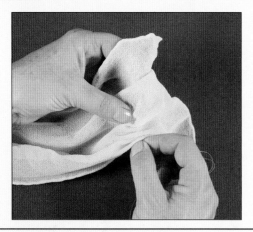

2 Create gathers by pulling the cut ends of the sewing thread. Make knots at both ends of each thread so the gathers remain intact during the dye process.

3 Place approximately 100ml acid dye with 1 tablespoon white vinegar in a locking baggie. Immerse the tied scarf in the dye.

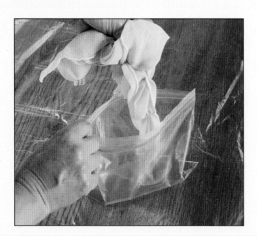

4 Place the baggie in a steam pot. Steam for 30 minutes to set the dye, keeping the temperature no higher than 185°F (85°C). When the scarf has cooled, carefully remove the stitches and rinse the scarf in warm water.

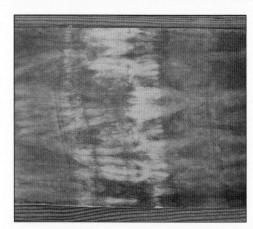

SCRUNCH TECHNIQUE

1 Fill a 1-pint Mason jar one-third of the way full with dye solution (approximately 200ml) and add 1 tablespoon white vinegar. Place one or two silk scarves in the jar. Stuff them in one at a time, creating random folds in the fabric as you go.

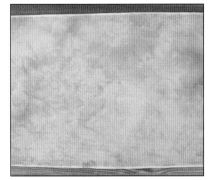

2 Pour 100ml of a contrasting color dye (this can be another leftover dye) over the scarves in the jar. Use a plastic fork to gently press down on the scarves to make the dye travel within the folds.

3 Steam the jar with the scarves using the steam pot with the rack for Mason jars. Monitor the temperature, keeping it at 185°F (85°C) for 30 minutes.

4 When the jar has cooled, rinse the scarves in warm water.

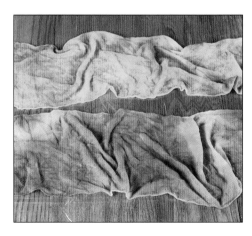

CONTINUED ON NEXT PAGE

FOLDED PLEATS

1 Using the silk setting on an iron, press the scarves to remove all wrinkles.

2 Make a 1-inch fold lengthwise and press the scarf along this fold.

3 Turn the scarf over and make a second fold lengthwise. Press this fold to form a pleat.

4 Continue to fold and press the scarf, forming crisp accordion pleats.

5 Create the resist pattern by tying cotton strings tightly at 2-inch intervals for the length of the scarf. Wherever you tie the string, the fabric will resist the second color.

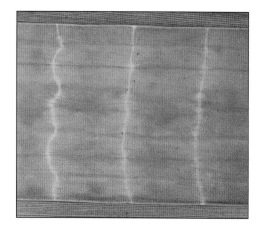

6 Place the scarf in a zipper-locked baggie with dye and vinegar, as described for the stitch and gather method. Place the baggie in a pot to steam for 45 minutes. When the pot has cooled, rinse the scarf in warm water, then remove the ties and rinse once again.

BOUND RESIST

1 Tie thin cotton string around glass marbles placed beneath the scarf. This creates bubbles and puckers in the silk fabric. You need about 20 marbles for an 11-×-60-inch scarf. Space the marbles at intervals to form a design.

2 Place the scarf in a zipper-locked baggie with dye and vinegar and steam as described above.

3 When the scarf is cooled, remove the ties and marbles and rinse in warm water. The marbles form a pattern resembling flowers or diamonds on the fabric.

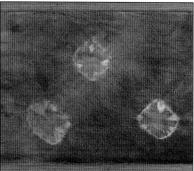

Here are some common problems dyers may experience and some suggested solutions.

PROBLEM: SOLID-SHADE DYE BATH IS UNEVEN AND STREAKY.

- **Solution 1:** Make sure you have thoroughly combined all dye bath ingredients.
- **Solution 2:** Make sure you are lifting the fiber and stirring the dye bath as the temperature increases.
- **Solution 3:** Be certain all dye powder is dissolved when creating dye solution.
- **Solution 4:** Make sure you have added Glauber salt to the dye bath.

PROBLEM: FIBER HAS DARK OR LIGHT SPOTS.

- **Solution 1:** Make sure figure-8 ties are loose enough for dye to penetrate.
- **Solution 2:** Make sure yarn or roving does not touch the bottom of the pot.
- **Solution 3:** Make sure you stir the dye bath while temperature rises.

PROBLEM: ACID DYE BATH DID NOT EXHAUST.

- **Solution 1:** Make sure you did not use more dye powder than needed for the amount of fiber.
- **Solution 2:** Make sure you added citric acid crystals to the dye bath.
- **Solution 3:** If you are nearing the end of a dye bath and see that there is quite a bit of unabsorbed dye, remove the fiber from the pot, add 2 tablespoons citric acid crystals or 1 cup white vinegar, return the fiber to the pot, and simmer for another 30 minutes.

PROBLEM: ROVING OR WOOL LOCKS BECAME FELTED IN THE DYE POT.

- **Solution 1:** Handle hot, wet fiber as little as possible. Never agitate fiber in the dye pot.
- **Solution 2:** Do not let the dye bath reach a rolling boil.

PROBLEM: YARN SKEINS BECAME TANGLED IN THE DYE POT.

- **Solution 1:** Be sure you have used at least 3 loose figure-8 ties on each skein.
- **Solution 2:** Use a shoestring tie looped through all skeins.

Disposing of Acid Dye Baths

Acid dye baths should be exhausted before disposal. Recapture any unexhausted dye leftover in the bath to dye small skeins of yarn, bits of fiber, or blank silk scarves. Keep some small skeins, hanks of roving, or fabric on hand in the event that you need to exhaust a bath. Add the fiber to the dye bath and bring to a simmer. Maintain the simmer until the dye bath is clear—at least 30 minutes.

Exhausted acid dye baths must be neutralized before disposal. Slowly add baking soda, a teaspoon at a time, until the dye bath pH reads close to 7 (neutral) on a pH test strip. Pour the bath down the drain, with lots of water.

chapter 7

Hand-Paint Variations

Hand-painting is the process of applying dye directly to fiber and then steaming the fiber to set the dye. The term *hand-paint* encompasses a range of techniques that create a variety of results. In some methods, you paint the dye onto yarn or roving using brushes. In other techniques, you do the "painting" with squeeze bottles or dip the fibers directly into containers of dye. You can hand paint variegated designs with a distinct repeating color pattern, or you can paint in a looser fashion, allowing adjacent colors to merge. Let your final project and desired effect dictate your method and color choices. Hand painting is exciting and fun. There are many ways to experiment with colors and patterns.

SET UP

Each hand-paint technique uses different tools for applying color to fiber. All methods described in this chapter require heat to set the dye. This is easily done by wrapping dyed fiber or yarn in plastic, rolling the packets into loose coils and placing them in an enamel canning pot converted to a steam chamber. To set up a steam chamber, place the wire canning rack in the bottom of the pot and cover it with an inverted Pyrex pie plate. Add water to just below the level of the pie plate. Place the coils of fiber on the pie plate (as shown) and cover the pot with a lid.

Protect your work surface by spreading a plastic covering on your painting table. Keep plenty of sponges and paper towels handy.

Unless otherwise instructed, prepare your dyes the day before your dye session so they will be room temperature when used. Hot dye solutions strike quickly. For all processes described in this chapter, you will soak your fibers in an acid presoak to wet out your fibers. The directions for creating an acid presoak are given below and were discussed in Chapter 4. This step alters the pH of the fiber so it can accept the dye (see **Note** below). In some instances, you may need to add acid to the dye solutions.

To make the presoak sufficient for 1 pound (454g) of fiber, add 12 tablespoons citric acid crystals and 4 teaspoons (10ml) Synthrapol to 2 gallons of warm 95°F (35°C) water. Stir to combine.

Note: *An acid presoak can be reused and stored indefinitely if you keep a lid on the bucket. If you ever need to add water, you may also need to add more citric acid crystals to maintain the proper acidity level. Check the acidity of a stored presoak solution using pH test papers. Tear a strip of paper from the roll and swish it in the solution. Then match the color with the guide. The pH of the acid soak should be in the range of 3–4.*

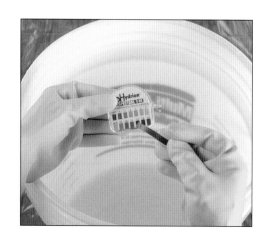

SAFETY

Be sure to review the safety guidelines in Chapter 2 and the complete instructions for making dye solutions in Chapter 5 before starting any dye procedure. Wear an apron to protect clothing, gloves and safety glasses to protect your skin and eyes, and a mask when handling dye powder and steaming fiber. Good lighting and good ventilation are important. However, when you are mixing dye powders, be sure to keep fans off and windows closed until the powders are safely dissolved in the solution. Always take care when working with hot pots.

When steaming successive batches of fiber, you will need to add more water to the pot. Check the water level before steaming a batch of fiber. Try to avoid lifting the lid while steaming. If you need to check the fiber or water level while steaming, always wear oven mitts and be careful not to get burned by the steam when you lift the lid. Never open plastic packets of fiber while they're still hot. You can easily get burned by the steam trapped inside the packets.

Safety Checklist

- Dust filter mask (when mixing dye powder)
- Dual cartridge respirator (when steaming)
- Rubber gloves
- Safety glasses
- Apron
- Vent fan while steaming fibers
- Oven mitts
- Good ventilation

Tricks for Controlling Dye Application

When hand painting yarn and fiber, there are times when you will want colors to remain clear and distinct and times when you will want more subtle color transitions. Sometimes dyes run together where two colors meet. This is called a *color bleed*, and it can be an attractive design feature in the yarn. If you don't want your colors to run, there are several ways to make them stay put. The following suggestions help you achieve the results you want.

Maintain Distinct Colors

USING DYE THICKENERS

Several products can be used to thicken dyes. Dye thickener stops colors from bleeding. They add an extra step and expense to the process, and you must wash the fibers thoroughly after dyeing to remove all traces of the thickener.

Guar gum and sodium alginate are thickeners that can be added to dye solutions. The more thickener you add, the less the color will bleed.

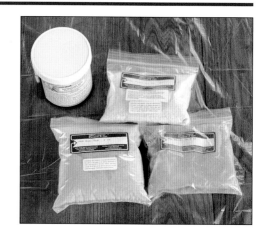

Guar gum and sodium alginate come in powdered form. They must be thoroughly mixed with water before use and work best if made at least one day in advance. Guar gum works with acid dyes and sodium alginate is used with fiber-reactive dyes.

Superclear (sold by Dharma Trading Company) is a ready-made thickening product that is colorless.

Follow the supplier's instructions for using thickeners, as the usage varies for each product.

USING RESISTS

A *resist* is a material used to mask areas of yarn or fiber that you want to preserve as undyed. When dyeing yarn or roving, you can use the type of resist tape sold for tie-dyeing fabric. Tightly bind and tie the sections of the roving or yarn that are to remain undyed and then apply color to the rest of the skein or hank. The resist tape can remain on the fiber right through the steaming process.

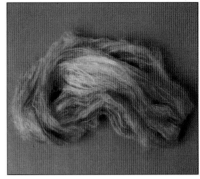

OTHER TIPS

Working on dripping-wet yarn increases the likelihood that the colors will run together and become muddy. Use the spin cycle on your washing machine to remove excess water from the fiber after the presoak. Let the fiber sit for 5 minutes before applying colors. The fiber will still be damp, but when you paint on the color (especially if you use a foam brush), the colors will stay put.

Adding citric acid crystals to the dye solution increases acidity and causes the dye to strike as soon as it makes contact with the fiber. For some of the processes described in this chapter, you will add acid directly to the dyes.

Throughout the following exercises, I emphasize the importance of mopping up pools of excess dye and blotting fiber before wrapping in plastic to steam. If there is too much dye on the fiber, the colors will run together in the steaming process, or you may get dark blotches where excess dye has pooled.

Allow Colors to Blend

When adjacent colors interact in hand-painted fiber, the results can be surprisingly lovely, since new colors emerge wherever two colors interact. Here are some ways to encourage that effect:

- Make sure the two adjacent colors form an appealing color when they blend. If red and green overlap to make brown, for example, is that really what you want?

- Do not remove quite as much water from the skeins after the soak. The water will allow the colors to spread a bit more.

- Paint adjacent colors close together or overlap adjacent colors.

- Keep a spray bottle of water on your worktable. Lightly spray the fiber to encourage colors to bleed.

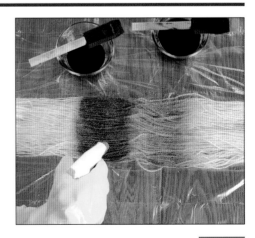

Plan Color Patterns and Palettes

The realm of hand-painting holds many possibilities for color combinations. Color choice and method of application are important ingredients in the recipe for any fiber project. The following pages offer suggestions for planning hand-paint projects.

Design a Hand-Painted Yarn

MAKE A TEST SWATCH

When hand-painting yarn, you must consider the gauge of the yarn, its intended use, and the desired color effect. These factors may influence your color choices and the method in which you apply them. Whenever possible, make a sample skein and knit a test swatch in the gauge of your final project to make sure you're satisfied with how the color pattern translates into the stitch pattern and gauge.

STRIPING YARN

If you want to create a pair of socks, a scarf, or a sweater from yarn that has horizontal color stripes in a repeating pattern, you will need to dye your yarn with color repeats of sufficient length to knit at least two rows of the pattern. For a pair of socks made from fingering-weight yarn, that means painting bands of color that are at least 60 inches (23.6cm) long. Painting self-striping yarn for a sweater would be very tricky, since the yardage needed to knit two rows would be considerably more.

Note: Consider the yarn gauge when determining length of color repeats. The smaller the gauge, the shorter the bands of color.

PLAN A COLOR PATTERN

When planning a color pattern, consider the number of colors, the circumference of the skein (in order to determine how long to paint each color segment), how long a pattern repeat will be, and how many pattern repeats there will be in one circle of the skein. In Chapter 4, I suggest winding skeins of 2-yard circumference (72 inches). This dimension makes it easy to work the numbers for color segments using repeats of 3, 4, 6, 8, 9, or 12 inches, since 72 is divisible by these numbers. In the diagram to the right, I use 4-inch segments (or bands) of three colors: blue, red, and green. This creates a 12-inch color pattern repeat, and there are six full repeats in the skein. The pattern is designed to be painted "around the skein," meaning that the color sequence "blue, red, green" repeats continually around the skein's circumference with no variation in color order. Painting yarn in this way creates a color rhythm that will carry throughout the garment design.

Some dyers prefer to paint across the skein. Use this method to paint a series of skeins at once, placed side by side. Paint color stripes that run across both sides of each skein. Keep in mind that this method alters the color progression. The skein in the figure to the right has a color pattern (from left to right) of blue, red, green, blue, red, green, blue, red, green, red, blue, green, red, blue, green, red. The colors in this skein stack up a little differently in knitting, so you should sample the skein to be sure you like the effect.

CONTINUED ON NEXT PAGE

**3-Color Pattern
Painting Around the Circumference
of a Skein**

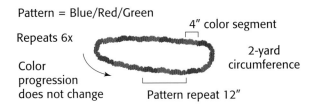

Pattern = Blue/Red/Green

Repeats 6x

4" color segment

2-yard circumference

Color progression does not change

Pattern repeat 12"

**3-Color Pattern
Painting Across the Skeins**

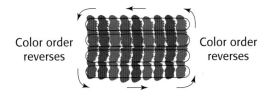

Color order reverses

Color order reverses

Color progression:
red | blue | green • red | blue | green • red | blue | green
green | blue | red • green | blue | red • green | blue | red

REPEATING DASHES OF COLOR

To achieve a dappled repeating color pattern in any knit garment, you can paint the yarn with shorter color bands to make an overall shorter pattern repeat. Yarns painted with color bands of approximately 3–4 inches will have a successive migration of color across each row. This can be quite attractive in plain stockinette or in lace patterns.

A WORD ABOUT POOLING

Pooling is a side effect or a design feature of hand-painted yarns, depending on how you look at it. Pooling refers to the blotching effect that occurs when colors stack up in a knitted swatch or garment to form pools of the same color. Pooling sometimes appears in a zigzag lightning pattern and sometimes appears in an amoeba-like fashion. Either way, the colors create a pattern that may or may not be appealing. Consider the end use of your hand-painted yarn when planning your colors. Be consistent in your color pattern (if pooling occurs, it will create a pattern rather than be a series of random color blotches). Knit a sample to test your color pattern before dyeing a large quantity of yarn. Chapter 11 offers tips for knitting with hand paints to thwart pooling.

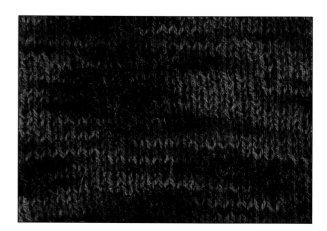

Color Effects

Analogous colors produce harmonious effects. Try widening an analogous palette to include one or more adjacent hues. For example, expand a blue/green colorway to include violet or yellow.

Consider color proportion. If you want a particular hue to be dominant, you can either paint longer bands of this color or repeat this color more often in the pattern sequence. Plum and lilac are the dominant colors in this roving, with accents of olive and smokey blue.

Vibrant contrasting colors can be quite striking in hand-painted yarns. This is achieved by placing complements side by side. However, if the bands of color are too short, the colors may dull each other when knit, woven, or spun.

Work with colors of similar value to avoid a yarn that has a spotty or "jumpy" appearance (see the discussion of value in Chapter 5). In the upper skein, the colors are close in value. There is greater contrast between darks and lights in the lower skein.

CONTINUED ON NEXT PAGE

Roving Color Planning

Many of the concepts for planning hand-painted yarns also apply to painted roving. Since roving is used to spin yarn, it is one step further removed from the finished product. So there are slightly different considerations to take into account when painting roving.

The roving and yarn shown here were dyed using the same colors (dark gray, silver blue-gray, and green) in the same pattern. The length of the color bands is approximately the same in both. If knit in stockinette on US8 needles, the yarn color changes approximately every 20 stitches (4–5 inches). The roving, depending on how it is spun, can become a yarn with either very long bands of colors or very short bands of colors. This depends on the thickness of the roving when you strip it down for spinning (See Chapter 11). It is much easier to create a long-striping yarn by dyeing roving and then spinning the yarn than it is to create long stripes by dyeing the yarn (as you will see in the self-striping sock exercise).

PURE BANDS OF COLOR

If you wish to spin a yarn that has pure bands of color that repeat in a pattern, you need to dye a roving with repeating bands of distinct color. The length of the color repeats depend on how often you wish the colors to change and how the yarn is spun. The roving on the left has 3–4 inch bands of color. Yarn spun from this roving has shorter bands of color. The roving on the right has 10–12 inch lengths of color, which translate into much longer color bands in the spun sample.

SPLASHES OF COLOR

For splashes of color that change quickly as the fiber is spun into yarn, colors can be applied in a painterly fashion to create color constellations rather than in bands. This is effective when the white background of the roving is used as a backdrop for the colors. Or you can create a pale color background by soaking the roving in a pale dye solution and then apply the dashes of different colors.

OTHER CONSIDERATIONS WHEN DYEING ROVING

When selecting colors for dyed roving, consider how colors will interact as the fibers are spun. In spinning, fibers are drafted before twist is added. *Drafting* is the process of drawing out fibers to a particular thickness for creating yarn of a certain diameter. Adjacent colors will blend and become diffused where they meet.

Analogous colors blend in a harmonious way, creating secondary colors.

Adjacent complementary colors may become muddy since they will mix as the fibers are drafted. This blending is called *optical mixing* (see Chapter 5).

To have a visually balanced yarn, use colors of similar value. Weaker shades of color will be overpowered by dominant, deeper shades. Dark and light fibers in the same roving can create a barber-pole effect when twisted together as yarn. This is not always an attractive feature.

Different fibers absorb dyes differently. For example, when dyeing silk top and wool top using the same dyes, the silk may appear lighter than the wool. You need stronger dye solutions to dye the silk to the same depth of shade as the wool. This is true of silk whether it is in yarn or roving.

 TIP

Consider the staple length (see Chapter 3) of the fibers when hand-painting roving. The relationship between staple length and the length of the color bands within a repeating color pattern determine how pure the colors will remain when spun. If the color bands are just a bit longer than the fiber staple, the colors will remain pure and intact when spun. If the color bands are shorter than the staple length, the colors will feather a bit more into each other as they are drafted and spun.

Paint Yarn with Foam Brushes

In this process, you paint the dye directly onto the yarn with foam brushes to create variegated skeins. Using wool skeins with a 2-yard circumference, this technique shows how to paint skeins with distinct 6-inch color bands that form an 18-inch color pattern repeat. The color pattern repeats four times around the circumference of the skein. Using dye thickener helps maintain distinct colors.

MATERIALS

- 4 four-ounce skeins (454g) of wool yarn, prepared for dyeing (see Chapter 4)
- 1 envelope each color Cushing Perfection Dyes: Plum, Mulberry, Rust
- Citric acid crystals
- Superclear dye thickener
- Synthrapol

TOOLS

- Pyrex measuring cup
- Measuring spoons
- 4 small plastic cups or containers for holding dye
- Permanent felt-tip marker and ruler for marking length of color bands
- Plastic wrap
- 4 two-inch-wide foam brushes
- Sponges and paper towels
- Enamel canning pot with rack and lid
- Pie plate to cover rack
- Small plastic bowl

SAFETY

Please review the safety guidelines at the beginning of this chapter and in Chapter 2; also review the instructions for mixing dye solutions in Chapter 5.

PREPARE TO DYE

1 Wet out the skeins in an acid presoak, following the instructions on page 94. Soak the skeins for a minimum of 30 minutes.

2 Mix the dye solutions in advance and allow them to reach room temperature before use. Mix each envelope of dye powder with 4 cups (1,000ml) boiling water, following the directions for mixing dye in Chapter 5.

3 You will paint one skein at a time. Spread two sheets of plastic wrap side by side, overlapping the plastic by 2 inches. The sheets should extend roughly 6 inches longer than the length of the skein.

4 Pour each dye solution into its own cup and place the cups in the order of your planned color sequence. You will use a separate foam brush for each color. Place the brushes beside each container.

Note: Keep your table clean as you work, wiping up any spills immediately. Place a damp sponge beside each cup to catch drips of dye.

5 Add 4 tablespoons (60ml) Superclear thickener to each dye solution and stir.

6 Using a ruler and a felt-tip permanent marker, make indicator marks on the plastic wrap, about 6 inches apart. These marks will guide your color application.

CONTINUED ON NEXT PAGE

7 Lift the wet skeins from the soak and gently press out the water. Place them in the spin cycle of a top-loading washing machine for 1 minute, without adding water. Excess water in the skeins can dilute the dye solution, so it's best to have the skeins damp but not wet.

8 Place one skein on the sheet of plastic wrap, spreading out the skein to form an oval. The two halves of the skein should not touch.

PAINT THE SKEINS

1 Saturate a foam brush with dye solution. Apply the color to create the first band in the color sequence. Use short downward strokes to apply the dye. You may need to apply more dye to the brush to fully cover one segment of the skein. The dye will not completely penetrate to the side of the skein facing down on the table. Don't worry; you will eventually turn the skein over to paint the other side.

2 Paint the next band of color, using a fresh brush for the second color. Leave a small white space between color bands so as not to contaminate the brush. Continue painting 6-inch segments of color, working your way around the skein's circumference. Maintain the color pattern—Mulberry, Plum, Rust—without changing the color sequence.

TIP

As the foam brushes make contact with the wet fiber, they absorb water. To avoid diluting the dye solution, press the brush into a dry rag or paper towel to blot after applying color to yarn.

3 Wipe up any drips or excess dye that runs from the skeins with a sponge.

4 Carefully lift the skein from one end. If there is a pool of dye beneath the skein, wipe it away with a paper towel.

5 Gently flip the skein over in order to paint the other side. Apply color with foam brushes following the same sequence.

6 Go back and gently touch up the white spaces where two colors meet. I sometimes use a small syringe for this step.

7 Wipe up any excess dye from the plastic wrap with a sponge. Blot the skein with paper towels to absorb any excess dye.

8 Create a packet by folding the ends of the plastic inward over the skein's ends and then folding the plastic lengthwise over the skein's sides. Do this for the top and bottom. To keep the color bands from making contact with each other, press down on the plastic to form a seal in the center between the two halves of the skein. Follow the same steps for the remaining skeins, folding each into its own plastic packet.

9 Loosely roll each packet from end to end.

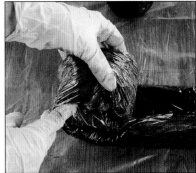

CONTINUED ON NEXT PAGE

STEAM THE SKEINS

1 Place the canning rack in the bottom of the enamel pot. Add about 2 inches of water to the pot, bringing the level just beneath the top of the rack. Make sure that the water level is sufficient for steaming, but that it doesn't come up to the level of the yarn.

2 Place the pie plate upside down over the rack. The pie plate prevents the boiling water from reaching the yarn during steaming. Excess water that escapes from the packets while steaming can run down the pie plate and drain into the bottom of the pot.

3 Set the plastic-wrapped packets of yarn on top of the pie plate inside the pot. Stand the packets on their side so the steam is distributed evenly to all parts of the skeins. Do not let the packets touch the side of pot. Cover the pot.

4 Bring the water to a simmer and maintain that temperature for 45 minutes. Halfway through the steaming time, turn the plastic packets upside down. This will help prevent any excess dye in the bottom of the packets from forming dark blotches on the yarn. Use caution when removing the lid from the pot (hot steam will escape), and wear oven mitts when handling the hot fiber.

5 At the end of 45 minutes, the dye has bonded with the fiber. Allow the pot of skeins to cool completely. Never attempt to open a hot package of yarn.

6 Remove the packets from the pot and carefully unwrap them. The skeins will have absorbed every bit of the dye, and there will be little liquid remaining in the packet.

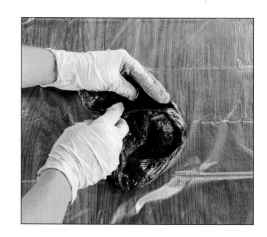

RINSE AND HANG TO DRY

7 Fill a basin with warm water. Add ½ teaspoon (2.5ml) Synthrapol. Soak the skeins for 5 minutes to remove any excess dye.

8 Create a second tepid bath and submerge the skeins to rinse completely.

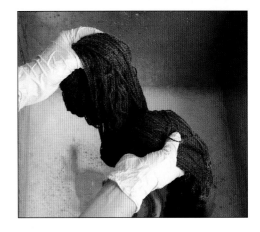

9 Remove excess water from skeins either by gently pressing or by spinning out in the washing machine. Doing so will speed the drying time.

10 Hang the skeins to dry on a rack or pole, out of direct sunlight.

Paint Semisolid Skeins

Use foam brush painting to create subtle value shifts of one color in a repeating pattern. This exercise shows you how to create a semisolid striation using dye stock made from two strengths of the same color for monochromatic skeins. Shimmering silk yarn provides the dramatic background, enhancing this technique.

MATERIALS AND TOOLS

- 8 two-ounce skeins 12/2 silk yarn wound in skeins measuring 69 inches in circumference; tied and prepared for dyeing (see Chapter 4)
- WashFast Dye Plum 822
- Citric acid crystals
- Synthrapol
- Superclear dye thickener
- Measuring cups and spoons
- Foam brushes
- Plastic wrap
- Canning pot with lid and rack for steaming skeins

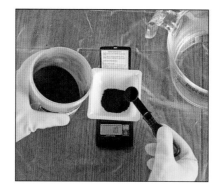 

PREPARATION

1 Presoak the silk skeins in the citric acid solution for at least 1 hour. (See Chapter 4 for instructions.)

2 Mix a 1% dye solution using 10g dye powder in 4 cups (1,000ml) boiling water (left photo). This will be the predominant value and the deeper color.

3 Prepare a 1% solution. 0.1% dye stock for a paler color value. Add 100ml of the 1% dye stock (created in Step 2) to 900ml of water (right photo).

PAINT THE SKEINS

To create a value striation, paint the skeins using a 2:1 ratio of dark-to-light values. Spread a damp skein in an oval on the table and, using a ruler and a permanent felt tip marker, measure and mark intervals on the sheet of plastic working your way around the skein's circumference. The circumference of the skein will determine the exact length of each section. For my skein, each repeat section is 9:4.5 inches.

Pour 1 cup (250ml) of each solution into a smaller cup and add 4 tablespoons (80ml) of Superclear to thicken the dye. Begin painting the 4½-inch sections using the lighter value.

Now paint the long 9-inch sections using the dark value. Be sure the dye penetrates evenly and covers every strand. Mop up any excess dye to avoid dark spots on the skein. Wrap the skein in plastic to steam, following the instructions in "Paint Yarn with Foam Brushes," see page 107. When steaming silk, monitor the temperature and do *not* allow it to go higher than 185°F.

When cool, remove the skeins from the plastic wrap and rinse in tepid water. Hang the skeins on a rack to dry, avoiding direct sunlight.

Dip-Dyed Yarn

Dip-dyeing creates a repeating color sequence with more diffused transitions. Rather than applying color with brushes, you apply color to the skeins by dipping them into containers of dye mixed with acid. I especially like this method for silk yarn. Sometimes it is easier to dye a tightly twisted silk yarn to the core by submersing rather than painting with dye. It is easier to manipulate skeins of smaller circumference with this technique.

MATERIALS

- 8 two-ounce skeins spun silk, wound in 54-inch circumference, tied and prepared for dyeing (see Chapter 4)
- Cushing Perfection Dye in three colors: Dark Gray, Silver Gray, Silver Gray Green
- Citric acid crystals
- Synthrapol

TOOLS

- 4-cup (1,000ml) Pyrex measuring cup and measuring spoons
- 3 two-quart (2L) plastic containers for holding dye
- Plastic wrap
- Sponges and paper towels
- Thermometer
- Enamel canning pot with rack and lid
- Pyrex pie plate
- Small plastic bowl
- Plastic shower curtain rings for manipulating skeins (two per skein)

SAFETY

Please review the safety guidelines at the beginning of this chapter and in Chapter 2; also review the guidelines for mixing dye solutions in Chapter 5.

PREPARE TO DYE THE SKEINS

1. Place the silk skeins in an acid presoak (see instructions on page 94).

   Note: It takes more time to wet out silk fiber. Allow the skeins to soak for a minimum of 1 hour, preferably longer.

2. Prepare your dye solutions, following the directions and precautions described in Chapter 5. Mix each envelope of dye powder with 4 cups (1,000 ml) boiling water. In this process, you want the dye to strike quickly, so it's better to make your solutions just before use, allowing them to cool slightly. Warm dye solutions will bond more quickly with fiber.

3. Spread two sheets of plastic wrap, slightly longer than the length of the skeins, on the table. The strips of plastic should overlap by about 2 inches.

4. Pour the dye solutions into the plastic tubs. Add 1 teaspoon citric acid crystals to each container and stir.

   Note: Adding citric acid crystals to the dye makes the dye strike the fiber more quickly.

THE DYEING PROCESS

1. Remove the skeins from the soak and gently press out water. You may place them in the washing machine on the spin cycle for 1 minute to remove all excess water.

2. Place two plastic rings on a skein. The rings become handles while dip-dyeing and will help you keep your gloves clean while maintaining control of the skein.

CONTINUED ON NEXT PAGE

Dip-Dyed Yarn *(continued)*

③ Dip one-third of the skein (about 18 inches) into the first color. Hold and swish the skein in the solution to allow the fiber to grab the dye.

④ Lift the skein and allow the excess dye to drip back into the container. Then gently press out excess dye.

⑤ Rotate the skein by repositioning the two rings. Dip the next third of yarn into the second color.

⑥ Lift the skein and allow the dye to drip back into the container. Gently squeeze out excess dye.

⑦ Repeat the dipping process for the last color on the last third of the skein. Set the dyed skein on the sheet of plastic wrap and remove the plastic rings. Then repeat all steps for the remaining skeins.

Note: *In dip-dyeing, there is the tendency for colors to bleed together. Take care when dipping not to dip the dyed portion of one section when dipping the next color. This will help prevent the dye solutions from becoming contaminated by other colors.*

TIP

Even when using the rings, your gloves may become splattered with dye. To prevent staining the undyed yarn, keep a small bowl of water on your worktable. Dip your hands in it to rinse off your work gloves when changing from working with one color to another.

STEAM THE SKEINS

1 Wrap each skein in its own sheet of plastic by laying the skein in an oval with space in the center (so the colors don't touch). Fold the plastic over both sides of the skein and press the plastic in the center to form a seal.

2 Roll each plastic-wrapped skein into a loose coil.

3 Set up the enamel canning pot to steam the skeins, as described earlier in this chapter on page 94.

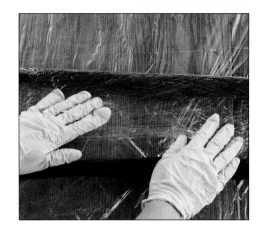

4 Place each skein on the pie plate inside the pot. Be sure the skeins have space around them and that they do not touch the side of the pot. You may have to steam half of the skeins at a time, to allow sufficient space for steam to circulate inside the pot.

5 Bring the water in the pot to a simmer and maintain the simmer for 45 minutes. Then allow skeins to cool inside the pot.

Note: Monitor temperature carefully when working with silk. Do not let the temperature rise beyond 185°F. Higher temperatures will destroy the silk's luster.

6 Carefully unwrap the skeins.

7 Rinse the skeins in a sink filled with warm water.

8 Gently press out excess water and hang skeins to dry, avoiding direct sunlight.

Use this process to create a space-dyed roving for handspinning. The painting is done with plastic squeeze bottles. The roving used in this demonstration is Wensleydale wool, which is long and lustrous. As mentioned in Chapter 3, you must take care when working with wet wool. If you handle the fibers too aggressively, they will felt. Subjecting wool to quick changes in temperature (for instance, placing hot fiber in a cool bath) can also cause felting.

MATERIALS

- 4 four-ounce hanks (454g) of wool roving tied into bundles with 2 shoelaces or plain cotton string (see Chapter 4)
- WashFast acid dyes in four colors: Plum 822, Chinese Red 307, Spiced Pumpkin 230, Reddish Brown 507
- Citric acid crystals
- Synthrapol

TOOLS

- 4-cup (1,000ml) Pyrex measuring cup
- Measuring spoons
- 4 eight-ounce plastic squeeze bottles
- Plastic wrap
- Sponges
- Paper towels
- Enamel canning pot with rack and lid
- Pyrex pie plate
- Rolling pin or 10-inch section of 1-inch-diameter PVC pipe (to distribute dye)
- Felt-tip permanent marker
- Ruler

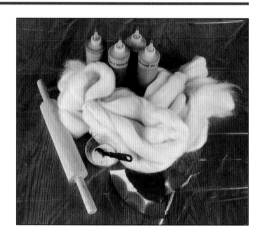

SAFETY

Please review the safety guidelines at the beginning of this chapter and in Chapter 2, and review the instructions for mixing dye solution in Chapter 5.

PREPARATION

1 Add the prepared bundles of roving to the acid presoak and gently press until all the fiber is submerged. Allow the fiber to soak for a minimum of 30 minutes. (See Chapter 4 for instructions to make an acid presoak.)

2 Prepare the dye solutions, referring to Chapter 5 for instructions and safety precautions. For each color, combine 10g dye powder with 4 cups (1,000ml) boiling water. Stir the solutions until all the dye has dissolved and allow solutions to cool to room temperature.

3 Dye each 4-ounce (114g) hank of roving in its own plastic-wrapped packet. Roll two long strips of plastic wrap onto the worktable. The plastic should be long enough to extend at least 3 inches beyond the length of the roving hank at both ends. The two strips of plastic should overlap by 2 inches where they meet in the center.

CONTINUED ON NEXT PAGE

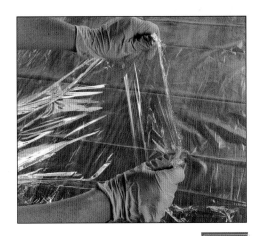

DYE THE ROVING

1 Pour the dye solutions into the plastic squeeze bottle.

2 Gently lift the bundles of the roving from the sink. Keep the roving together by supporting the mass of fiber with both hands so it doesn't drift apart.

3 Press excess water from the roving. You can spin it out in the washing machine, but handle the fiber carefully.

4 Remove the ties from the hank and arrange the roving in a zigzag fashion on the plastic wrap.

5 Using a ruler and a felt-tip permanent marker, mark the plastic to indicate the length of the color repeats.

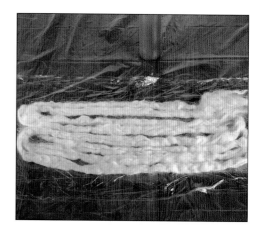

6 Apply the first color to the roving. Gently squeeze the bottle and squirt the color in a back-and-forth pattern working across the width of the hank. Distribute the dye evenly but don't worry now if there are white spots.

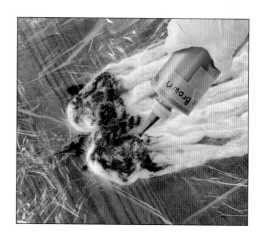

7. Carefully lift the roving and, using a paper towel, wipe away any dye that has pooled on the plastic underneath. Then turn the roving over so you can paint the other side.

8. Paint the other side of the roving, following the same process as before. You now need to decide if you want the spots of undyed white fiber to be a design feature. If the roving is to be solidly dyed, go back and apply a little more color to any large white spots, also paying attention to the places where two colors meet.

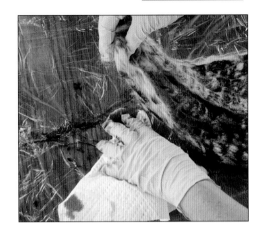

9. Cover the roving with another sheet of plastic. Use gentle pressure and a rolling pin to spread the dye more evenly.

10. Lift the sheet of plastic and blot up any excess dye with a paper towel. Fold the sides of the plastic over the fiber to form a sealed packet and roll the packet into a jellyroll. Paint the remaining hanks of roving in the same way.

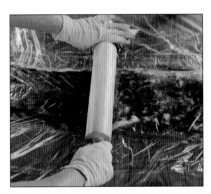

Steam the Fiber

1. Place 2 inches of water in the bottom of your enamel canning pot, set the rack inside, and place the pie plate upside down over the rack. Arrange your rolled packets inside the pot; make sure they do not touch the sides.

2. Bring the water in the pot to a simmer and steam the fiber for 45 minutes. Allow the pot to cool completely before removing the fiber packets.

3. Carefully unwrap the roving. Fill a sink with warm water and submerge the roving. Because the roving is no longer tied, be careful placing it in the soak. Allow it to sit for 2 minutes. You may push the fiber down, but do not agitate it!

4. The wet roving will be a tangled mass. Gently press out the excess water. Set it on a rack where the excess water can drip out. Once it has finished dripping, you can detangle it and hang it properly to dry.

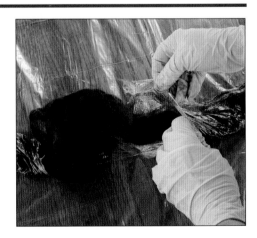

Self-Striping Sock Skeins

Long color repeats are the secret to creating the stripes. For smaller projects, such as socks or scarves, you can paint a yarn dyed in a succession of striping colors by using long segments of solid colors in very long repeats. The knitted garment appears to be knit from multiple yarns of different colors, but the color work is all done using a paint brush and some color planning. It takes at least two knitted rows in a sock to form a stripe—with each row using roughly 30 inches (76.2cm) of yarn. This demonstration dyes a mammoth skein of a wool and nylon blend yarn to create one pair of socks striped in four colors.

MATERIALS AND TOOLS

- Superwash sock yarn on a cone, approximately 1,700 yards/1 lb.
- WashFast dyes: Colonial Blue 401, Navy 413, Boysenberry 811, Lavender 812; 1 teaspoon (2.5g) of each color mixed with 1 cup (250ml) boiling water
- Superclear dye thickener
- Citric acid crystals
- Synthrapol
- White cotton string
- Warping board (see photo at right)
- Yardage counter
- 4 foam brushes
- Yarn ball winder
- Plastic wrap
- Enamel canning pot with lid and rack
- Pie plate
- 4 Pyrex measuring cups
- Sponges
- Paper towels

Warping board

Note: It's helpful to have a long table for painting this skein. Each band of color will be 4 yards long.

SAFETY

Follow the safety guidelines described at the beginning of this chapter and in Chapter 2. Refer to Chapter 5 for complete instructions for mixing dye solutions.

WIND THE SKEIN

Use a *warping board* (see Tip on page 122) to wind a 400-yard skein with a wide circumference (approximately 17 yards!). You need a skein of large circumference to paint multiple color bands of long lengths. Wind your skein from the cone as follows:

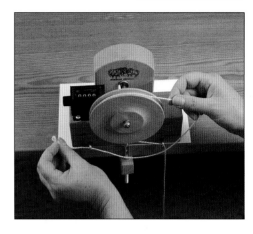

1 Form a loop in one end of the yarn and knot it. Thread the yarn through the yardage counter (see photo). Then place the loop over the peg in the upper-right corner of the warping board (peg #1 in diagram below). Your skein will begin and end here.

2 Begin to wind the skein running the yarn from peg #1 to peg #2 at the left side of the board. Go around peg #2 and run the yarn across the board again, wrapping around peg #3 on the right. Continue wrapping the yarn around each peg in succession as you go back and forth across the warping board. Keep a light, even tension, but do not stretch the yarn.

Winding Skein on Warping Board

——— = yarn   ✳ = choke ties • indicate color change

< = direction to wind   ✕ = extra ties to keep skein together

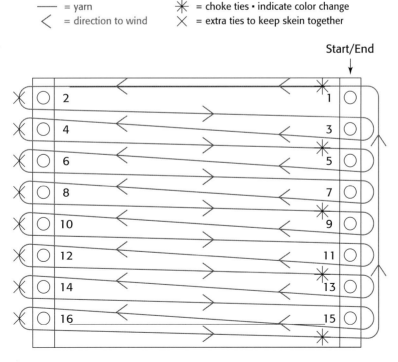

CONTINUED ON NEXT PAGE

③ When you reach the last peg in the lower-left corner (peg #16), wrap the yarn around the peg and then bring it from left to right along the outside of the board and back up along the pegs on the right side to where you started (see below left). This creates one full circumference of the skein.

④ Continue to wrap consecutive "laps," always following the same path with the yarn.

⑤ Keep your eye on the yardage counter. The skein will be 400 yards (366m)—enough for a pair of socks—but you will want to stop winding and place a marker at 200 yards (183m) so you will know where the second sock begins when knitting. Do this by tying a string around the skein when you reach 200 yards (183m) (see below right). Then continue to wind.

TIP

A *warping board* is a weaving tool that can come in handy for working with skeins. If you are trying this technique for the first time, you may be able to borrow a board from a member of your local weavers' guild. While most warping boards are approximately 1 yard wide, they can vary in number of pegs. You can use any warping board, even if it has fewer pegs than the one used here. If you have fewer pegs, your skein circumference will be smaller.

TIE THE SKEIN

Placing ties at set intervals keeps the long skein intact and indicates where color changes will occur. Each tie made on the right side of the warping board is a secure choke tie—a firm double knot—to keep the strands of yarn from sliding and becoming tangled. The choke ties are removed as you paint the skein, but they are necessary for keeping the skein under control until then. The choke ties will also indicate the places where you change color.

1 Place a tie around the second 200-yard (183m) portion of the skein, at peg #1. You now have ties separating the two halves of the skein. Then place a second tie around the entire skein at peg #1.

2 For this skein you will place the choke ties at approximately 4-yard intervals, which occur at every other odd-numbered peg on the right (see diagram). These ties indicate where colors will change. A 4-yard color segment will translate into roughly four knit rows in a stockinette sock pattern. Place a tie on peg #5. Continue to place consecutive ties on every other odd-numbered peg on the right side of the board (pegs 9, 13).

3 Your last choke tie equally divides the long run from peg #16 at the lower left to peg #1.

Place firm bow ties at each of the even-numbered pegs on the left side of the board. The bow ties do not indicate color changes. They will simply keep the skein in order.

4 Remove the skein from the warping board, one side at a time. Fold the skein back and forth upon itself and tie it in two places to hold it together.

CONTINUED ON NEXT PAGE

PREPARE TO DYE

1. Place the skein in an acid presoak for at least 30 minutes (see Chapter 4 for presoak instructions).

2. Make the dye solutions and allow them to cool. See Chapter 5 for guidelines for safely preparing dye solutions.

3. Add 4 tablespoons (80ml) Superclear thickener to each cup of dye solution. Mix thoroughly.

4. In this process you wrap each 4-yard band of color in its own swath of plastic wrap. Lay out a strip of plastic wrap approximately 4 yards long on the table. (If your table is not 4 yards long, spread a sheet of plastic wrap across the length of your table.)

5. Remove the skein from the presoak and gently squeeze out excess water.

6. Remove the two ties holding the folded skein together and arrange the skein on the table so the first band of color sets on the plastic wrap. Since you will only work on one portion of the skein at time, tuck the rest of the skein out of the way. (You can let it hang off the table; allowing it to rest on the floor is fine. You can place it in a plastic tub on the floor to keep it clean.) This will keep the undyed portion of the skein from becoming stained with dye.

PAINT THE SKEIN

1. Working from left to right, apply the dye with the foam brush. Use short strokes and be sure to coat all strands of yarn.

2 Place new ties around the freshly painted section at both ends. Once you have painted a full segment of color, use a sharp pair of small scissors to carefully snip the choke ties. Make sure you cut only the ties and not your yarn!

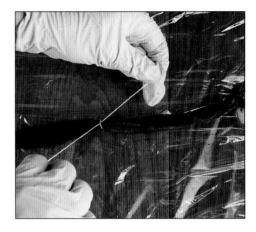

3 Wipe any excess dye from the plastic wrap. Then fold the plastic around the painted section of the skein.

TIP

Use short brush strokes rather than running the brush down the length of the skein. Use one hand to hold the yarn firmly on the table while the other hand brushes on the dye. Be sure to clean your gloves before handling the undyed portions of the skein.

CONTINUED ON NEXT PAGE

4 Shift the wrapped painted section to the right. Spread another swath of plastic on the table and lay the next unpainted section of the skein on the table.

5 Paint the second band with the next color.

6 Make a new choke tie around the painted area at the left side. Carefully snip the old choke tie at the color transition point at the left.

7 Wrap the second section in plastic, slightly overlapping where the two sections of plastic wrap meet.

8 Continue painting the skein. As you complete each section, rotate the skein around from left to right.

Work in sections, painting your way around the skein. Follow the same color sequence (in this case, the skein was painted Navy, Colonial Blue, Boysenberry, Lavender).

STEAM THE SKEIN

1. When all sections are painted and wrapped, fold the skein onto itself, roll it to form a coil, and place it in the pot to steam for 45 minutes.

2. Allow to cool completely. Working section by section, unwrap the plastic.

3. Make a warm rinse bath, adding ½ teaspoon Synthrapol to the water. Submerge the skein and swish gently to remove all traces of thickener. Rinse again in a clear warm bath. Spin out excess water and drape the skein over a rack or towel bar to dry.

WIND AND START KNITTING

1. Spread the skein out on the floor in a large oval. Carefully snip all the choke ties, but leave the two ties that divide the skein into two 200-yard (182.3m) skeins.

2. Holding a ball winder in your hand, snip the first tie and thread the end of the skein onto the winder. Walking in a circle, slowly reel the yarn onto the ball winder. Continue to walk around the circumference of the skein, reeling as you go, until you reach the tie that indicates you have wound half the skein (200 yards) into a ball.

3. When you reach this second tie, stop winding and remove the first ball from the winder. Cut the tie and thread the end of the second half of the skein and begin winding as you did for the first half of the skein.

4. When finished, you will have two nearly identical 200-yard (182.3m) balls. Each ball of yarn is enough to knit a sock.

Winding a very large self striping yarn skein into a ball on your living room floor

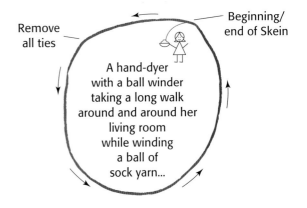

Knit your socks to see your self-striping pattern emerge. When you knit the second sock, be sure to start at the same end of the second ball of yarn (with the same color that started the first sock). When you are finished, you will have a perfectly matched pair.

Self-Striping Shortcut

Machine-knit, undyed sock blanks are a fun shortcut for painting self-striping sock yarn. *Sock blanks* are rectangular swatches knit in stockinette. Each blank is enough for knitting a pair of socks. (Some blanks are sold as singles, so you need to paint two that match for a pair of socks.) You paint your color stripes or pattern directly on the sock blank. Painting stripes on the fabric swatch gives you a good picture of how your finished sock will look. When you have set the dye, you knit directly from the swatch, unraveling as you go.

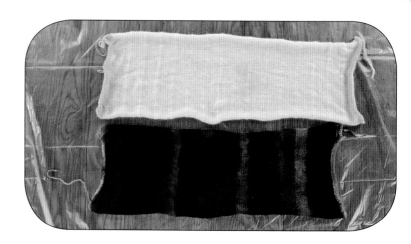

MATERIALS

- WashFast dyes: Colonial Blue 401, Navy 413, Boysenberry 811, Lavender 812; 1 teaspoon of each color mixed with 1 cup (250ml) boiling water
- Superclear dye thickener

TOOLS

- Wool sock blank
- 4 short-bristle stencil brushes or narrow stiff-bristle paintbrushes
- 4 Pyrex measuring cups
- Plastic wrap
- Paper towels
- Canning pot with lid and rack
- Pie plate
- Large styrofoam board and pushpins (for stretching out wet sock blank)

PREPARATION

1. Place the sock blank in an acid presoak (see page 94 for instructions). Allow it to soak for at least 1 hour in order to fully wet out the knitted swatch.

2. Prepare the four dye solutions following the guidelines in Chapter 5. Allow the solutions to cool before using.

TIP

Sock blanks have a tendency to curl at the edges. In this demonstration, I have pinned the sock blank to a piece of Styrofoam covered with plastic to keep the blank open and flat while painting. (This suggestion was made by Nancy Roberts of *Machine Knitting to Dye For*.)

③ Add 4 tablespoons (80ml) Superclear to each solution and stir to thicken the dye.

④ Spread a sheet of plastic wrap slightly longer than the sock blank on the table.

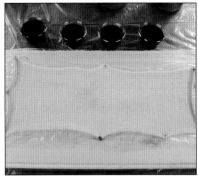

⑤ Remove the sock blank from the presoak. Gently press out the excess water, but do not wring the fabric. Lay the sock blank on the plastic wrap.

PAINT THE SOCK

Your pattern and stitch gauge may differ from the gauge of the sock blank, so your final result will not be identical to the stripes or pattern you paint on the sock blank. Plan your self-striping color design on paper in advance.

Note: Some sock blanks are a continuous rectangle. To make the sock pair match, find the midpoint and repeat the color pattern for the second sock once you reach the middle. Other blanks are in two sections, making it easy to see where one sock ends and another begins.

① Begin to paint the first stripe. Use a plastic ruler as a guide to define the color bands clearly. Press down with the brush to force the dye between the stitches, but do not agitate the surface of the swatch too vigorously. Pay attention to the edges of the swatch to make sure you leave no white spots.

② Wipe off the ruler and use it again as a guide to paint the second stripe. Place your colors close together, but do not overlap them. The dye thickener should inhibit color bleeding. If the colors do bleed, add more thickener to the dye.

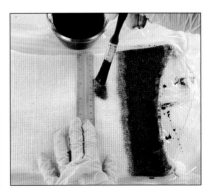

CONTINUED ON NEXT PAGE

3 Continue to paint your stripe design. If you are using the type of blank that is long enough for one pair of socks (such as the ones from Plymouth Yarns), you will need to repaint your design when you reach the halfway point of the blank. If you are using the style of blank shown here (from *Machine Knitting to Dye For*), you will paint a second blank, following the same pattern for the second sock.

4 Cover the painted sock blank with a paper towel and gently blot any excess dye. Lay another sheet of plastic over the blank and flip it over.

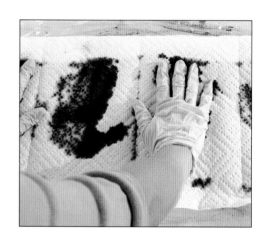

5 Lift the plastic from the reverse side of the blank. Quite likely, you will see many white spots where the dye did not penetrate. Apply dye to the reverse side, following your design. Make sure to cover any white spots along the edges.

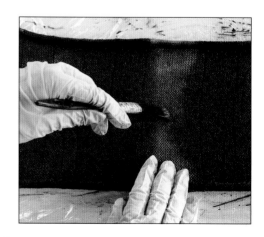

6 Blot gently with another paper towel and replace the plastic wrap.

7 Roll the edges of the two plastic sheets to form a seal. Allow the blank to sit for 10 minutes before steaming. This gives the dyes a chance to set.

Steam, Rinse, and Knit

1 Place the folded packet in the steamer and steam for 45 minutes. Allow the pot to cool before removing the swatch from the plastic.

2 Place the swatch in the sink with warm water and ½ teaspoon (2.5ml) Synthrapol. Swish gently to remove the thickener and excess dye.

3 Place the blank between two towels and gently press to blot the excess water. Block the swatch on a dry towel on a flat surface. Maintain the shape and do not stretch the fabric.

4 Most sock blanks have cotton waste yarn at one end to keep the swatch from unraveling. Start at that end and carefully remove the waste yarn.

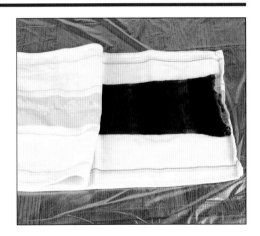

5 Unravel a row of dyed yarn and cast on following your knitting pattern. The yarn will be kinky, so your stitches may not lie flat. This unevenness will be addressed when you block the finished sock.

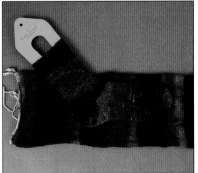

CONTINUED ON NEXT PAGE

Design Variations

Painting sock blanks is a bit like working on a canvas. The exciting part is seeing how your painted blank translates to a knitted sock. If you knit in stockinette, your result will more closely mirror the painted blank. Interesting results will emerge if you try different stitch patterns, but you must keep in mind the yardage of the blank, since you don't want to run out of yarn before you finish knitting your sock!

Experiment with geometric patterns. Using a thickener will give defined edges. It you want the colors to bleed, use less or no thickener in the dye.

For a watercolor effect, submerge the blank in a pot of water with approximately 1 cup (250ml) of pale dye solution. Once the swatch has absorbed the dye, blot out the excess water and paint a design over the pale background using foam stencil brushes. For a diffused effect, spray the blank lightly with a vinegar and water solution, then wrap and steam. Use resists to experiment with color and pattern. You can create interesting results using tie-dye techniques.

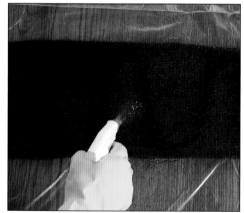

TIP

Sometimes you will find the knitted sock has a heathered look. This is because the dye didn't penetrate the stitches of the blank. For a more solidly dyed sock, try dyeing a sock blank in two steps. First, dye it in an immersion bath and let it soak up the color. Then paint colored stripes over the base color, following the steps described in this chapter.

If you enjoy knitting two socks at a time, try one of the sock blanks knit with two strands of yarn. These blanks (available from KnitPicks) provide the closest possible color-matched socks, because the strands of yarn for each sock are dyed side by side in the swatch.

Here are some issues you may encounter with various hand-painting techniques, and some suggested solutions.

Problem: You discover unintentional white spots after dyeing.

Solution 1: You can touch up your yarn or roving using dye left over from your hand painting. If the dye solution does not contain acid, add 1 teaspoon (5g) of citric acid crystals to the solution and stir. Using a foam brush, apply the color to the white spots and resteam the fiber.

Solution 2: Carefully inspect the yarn or roving for undyed spots before wrapping and steaming.

Problem: Colors continue to bleed in the aftersoak.

Solution 1: While it is normal to see some color in the initial rinse, if the dye continues to bleed from the fiber, then the color has not bonded with the fiber. Take a stockpot, add 3½ gallons of water and 1 tablespoon citric acid crystals (for 1 lb/454g of fiber), and bring the acid water to a simmer. Place the fiber in the pot and let it simmer for about 30 minutes.

Solution 2: Use a thermometer clipped to the side of your steaming pot while cooking the fiber. Make sure you allow enough time for the fiber to steam once it has reached the correct temperature. If you do not steam long enough, the dyes may not fully bond.

Solution 3: Make sure there is enough room for steam to travel in the steam pot. If there are too many packets of fiber crowded together in the pot, the heat may not be evenly distributed.

Problem: The colors bled together during the steaming process and are virtually indistinguishable.

Solution 1: You may have applied more dye than the fiber could absorb. Try using less dye next time. Also remember that you must blot up any excess dye before wrapping the fiber in plastic.

Solution 2: Try mixing a thickener into your dye solutions.

Solution 3: There may have been too much water left in the fiber from the presoak. Be sure to extract as much water as possible before dyeing.

Problem: There are dark splotches of color on the fiber.

Solution 1: Dark patches occur when dye pools beneath the yarn or roving while you are applying color. As you paint, you must lift the fiber and wipe away the excess dye that accumulates. Blot the entire skein or hank with paper towels to absorb any excess dye.

Solution 2: Once you have rolled your packets of fiber, poke small holes in the plastic so the excess dye can run out.

Solution 3: Colors can contaminate each other if they touch inside the packets. Wrap the fibers carefully so colors do not touch one another.

Solution 4: Try turning the packets of fiber once, halfway through the steam process. Wear hot mitts and be careful when lifting the pot lid during cooking.

Problem: In the process of dyeing a number of skeins (or hanks), the dye colors changed or lost their strength.

Solution: Colors change visibly when the solutions become contaminated by other colors. While this is bound to happen to some extent, you can minimize the effect by using one brush for each color and keeping your brushes from coming into contact with other colors. Keep your gloves clean, too—use a rinsing bowl and towel to clean your gloves when changing from one color to another.

Colors weaken when they become diluted with water. This may happen when painting with brushes or dip-dyeing. Be sure to blot any excess water from your foam brush after applying dye to the fiber. When dip-dyeing, be sure to spin excess water from the fiber before you begin painting.

8

Freestyle Dyeing

The dyeing techniques in this chapter are playful color experiments, applied freestyle, that yield random results. Sometimes the most interesting and exciting outcomes occur when you let your imagination take the lead.

The methods described in this chapter deviate from traditional modes of dyeing. In some cases, recipes and formulas do not apply. Many of the methods presented are great ways to use leftover dyes from other projects. As with any other dye process, sample first. Always test your results for colorfastness.

While there may or may not be repeating color patterns and the results may be difficult to replicate, projects created from these hand-dyed fibers are truly one of a kind.

Kool-Aid Slow Cooker Dyeing

Packets of unsweetened Kool-Aid (or similar powdered beverage products) contain all the ingredients you need for an acid dye bath: citric acid crystals and food coloring.

Slow cookers are perfect for simmering small batches of fiber. Because the fibers steep in a heated bath of color for a long time, the shades are deep and intense. Several colors added one at a time produce exciting results.

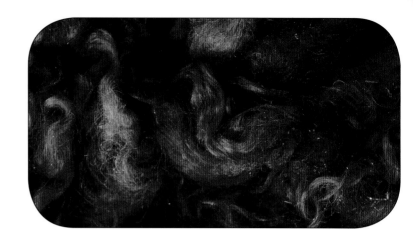

Slow Cooker Method

In the following demonstration, I use washed mohair locks to produce a basket of rainbow-dyed fiber for spinning. You can substitute similar amounts of wool locks, roving, or yarn for the same process.

Note: *While Kool-Aid dyeing is very safe, you must still follow safety guidelines for acid dyes (please review Chapter 2). Once you use a slow cooker for dyeing fiber, dedicate it to that purpose.*

MATERIALS

- Approximately 8 ounces (227g) Mohair locks, wetted out in advance
- Unsweetened Kool-Aid (or similar unsweetened powdered drink mix): 2 packages orange, 2 packages cherry, and 1 package grape

TOOLS

- Slow cooker dedicated to dyeing use
- Plastic spoon
- Pyrex measuring cup

1 Add ½ cup (125ml) water to the slow cooker (or enough to cover the bottom of the pot with 1 inch of water).

2 Mix 2 packages of orange Kool-Aid with 1 cup (250ml) room-temperature water.

3 Mix 1 package of cherry Kool-Aid with 1 cup (250ml) water.

4 Stack the damp mohair locks in the slow cooker. It's okay to crowd the pot since you will not stir this dye bath. Plug in the pot and set the temperature to high.

5 Start with the lightest color. Pour the orange dye slowly over one half of the fiber in the slow cooker. Place the lid on the pot.

6 Wait about 20 minutes, giving the pot time to heat and the fiber a chance to absorb the orange. Then add the cherry dye to other side of the pot, pouring slowly and evenly.

7 Wait 20 minutes more, then sprinkle 2 teaspoons of the cherry powder over the top of the pot using a plastic spoon. Replace the lid and let the fibers steep.

8 Wait another 20 minutes and then sprinkle 2 teaspoons of the grape powder lightly across the top of the pot. Replace the lid and let the pot simmer for an hour or until all the dye has been absorbed. The water should be clear at the end of the process.

9 Allow the pot to cool completely and then rinse the fiber.

Direct Pour Low Water Method

Dyeing in low water is similar to immersion dyeing because the fiber is immersed in a dye bath, but is also similar to hand-painting because you pour the colors directly onto the fibers while they simmer. Working with low water gives you some control over the application of color and the spread of the dye. Since there is less water, there is less opportunity for the dyes to migrate. They strike wherever they make contact with the fiber, producing beautiful results in a less controlled fashion.

Dye Roving in Low Water

This process creates a trio of rovings in related colors. I use a Cormo wool and Bombyx silk roving to add textural as well as visual interest. Silk and wool absorb dye differently, adding visual interest when the roving is spun into yarn. Yarn can also be used for this method.

Pay careful attention with fine wool to avoid felting. This process works best on a burner that gives you good control at low settings.

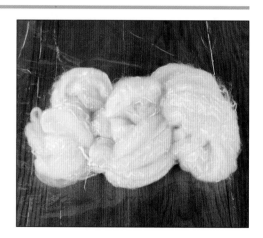

MATERIALS

- 12 ounces (227g) Cormo wool and silk-blend roving
- Citric acid crystals
- 250ml dye stock of each color WashFast: Reddish Brown, Plum, and Chinese Red

TOOLS

- 20-quart pot, wide and shallow
- Squeeze bottles
- Long-handled spoon or tongs
- Thermometer

PREPARATION

1 Divide the roving into three 4-ounce hanks and create tied bundles as described in Chapter 4. Place the roving in an acid presoak for at least 1 hour.

2 Prepare the dye stocks. For each color, mix 2.5g dye powder with 250ml boiling water. Allow the dye to cool before use.

3 You will dye each hank of roving separately. For the first roving, set 100ml of Reddish Brown, the main color, aside in a beaker. Pour the two accent colors, Plum and Chinese Red, into squeeze bottles and set aside.

4 To make the dye bath, pour 3L (3 quarts) room-temperature water into the pot. Add 2 teaspoons citric acid crystals and stir.

5 Add 100ml Reddish Brown dye stock to the pot. Stir to combine well.

6 Carefully remove the roving from the presoak and press out the excess water. Place the roving in the dye pot and gently press down to immerse the fiber.

7 Place the pot on the cooking surface over medium heat. Do not stir or agitate the roving. Check the water temperature continually with a thermometer—it will climb quickly since there is little water in the pot.

TIP

The roving may form a dome, trapping the heat beneath it. When you check the temperature, be sure to place the thermometer in the water beneath the roving. If heat is building up in the bottom of the pot, carefully lift the roving with a spoon or tongs to distribute the temperature evenly.

CONTINUED ON NEXT PAGE

APPLY THE DYE

1 The base color will begin to exhaust as the water temperature reaches approximately 160°F (71°C). You should notice the water in the bath turning clear, a sign that the dye has bonded with the fiber. Now you can begin to paint.

2 Apply thin ribbons of Chinese Red in a back-and-forth pattern over the surface of the roving. Be conservative in adding color. It's better to add too little rather than too much at first. The dye will strike wherever it lands. You do not want this color to disperse, so do not stir.

3 Monitor the temperature. Turn down the heat slightly as the water reaches 185°F.

Note: You do not want the temperature to exceed 185°F (85°C). A boiling temperature in a low water bath will felt the wool and ruin the luster of the silk.

4 When the second color has exhausted, you can add the next color. Apply dots of the Plum color in a random fashion. Applying the colors one at a time allows each color time to bond with the fiber. In some spots the colors will stay relatively pure, and in others the colors will merge to form new colors.

5 Carefully turn the roving using the spoon. Apply the colors to the other side.

6 Maintain the consistent temperature for 30 minutes. Then turn off the heat and allow the fiber to cool in the dye bath. The water will be clear.

Repeat the process to dye the remaining rovings. For the second roving, use Chinese Red as the main color in the dye bath with Plum and Reddish Brown as accent colors. For the third roving, try Plum as the main color with Chinese Red and Reddish Brown as accent colors.

RINSE AND DRY

1 Unspun silk fibers may easily drift apart when wet. Give the roving a gentle rinse in warm water and place on a flat drying rack to dry.

2 Gently separate and fluff out the roving once it's completely dry. When the yarn is spun, you will want to wash this fiber more thoroughly to remove any residual dye.

Dyeing Yarn in Low Water

Follow the same steps for dyeing yarn skeins in a low water dye bath. In a 20-quart shallow pot, you can dye two 4-ounce skeins. Use just enough water in the dye bath to cover the skeins. Turning the skeins halfway through the process will distribute the colors more evenly.

To prevent dye pooling, paint the dye in thin ribbons using the squeeze bottle application.

Spray-Paint Fiber

For this technique, use spray bottles to apply either a heavy or light mist of contrasting colors on undyed yarn or roving. When done lightly, this gives the fiber an airbrushed look. When sprayed more liberally, colors really pop against a white background. To avoid creating muddy colors, stick with two or three analogous hues when first experimenting with this technique.

Dye Roving by Spray-Paint Method

MATERIALS

- 8 ounces (227g) roving (wool and silk are used in this chapter)
- 3 spray bottles with adjustable nozzles
- 0.1% dye stock, 1 cup (250ml) of each of three colors (WashFast Reddish Brown, Slate Blue, and Plum)
- Acid soak solution (see Chapter 4): citric acid crystals and Synthrapol

TOOLS

- Canning pot with lid and rack
- Pie plate
- Plastic wrap

SAFETY

It's very important to wear a safety mask when using this method, as you will be spraying liquid dye onto the fiber. Be sure to follow all the guidelines described in "Safety Essentials" in Chapter 2.

> ## TIP
>
> Spray bottles with adjustable nozzles tend to spray heavier amounts of liquid, even on their finest setting. If you want a very light veil of color, use a fine mist spray bottle, available from the dye supply companies listed in the appendix.

PREPARATION

1 Prepare rovings in hanks and tie in bundles as described in Chapter 4. Place rovings in acid soak solution. Soak silk overnight in order for the acid solution to penetrate the roving.

2 Place dye stock in spray bottles.

3 Cover your work area with plastic sheets.

4 Extract roving from acid soak solution and gently press to remove excess water. Untie the bundle and arrange the roving on the plastic wrap. Carefully fan the roving out to create as much surface area as possible.

DYE THE ROVING

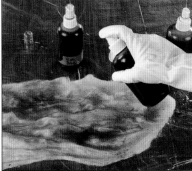

1 Use spray bottles to apply dyes. Beginning with the lightest color, lightly spray the roving. You can either spray a base layer over the entire surface or spray spots of color.

2 Allow the sprayed area to sit for at least 5 minutes before flipping the roving to spray the other side.

3 Flip the roving and repeat the process. Wipe any excess spray dye from the plastic wrap.

4 Allow the roving to sit for another 5 minutes before wrapping in plastic to form a packet.

5 Place the roving packets in the steaming pot and steam for 45 minutes. Monitor the temperature if you are dyeing silk or silk blends, maintaining a temperature of 185°F (85°C). Allow the fiber to cool completely before removing from the plastic.

6 Rinse the roving in warm water and hang to dry.

CONTINUED ON NEXT PAGE

Dye Yarn with the Spray-Bottle Method

Use the same process with minor adjustments to paint bursts of color on yarn. This technique works best with a chunky-weight yarn, such as a heavy worsted-weight wool. The colors used here are WashFast Peach Blossom and WashFast Periwinkle.

① Prepare the skeins by soaking them in the acid presoak. Spin the excess water out before dyeing, leaving the skeins slightly damp.

② Spread each skein on a sheet of plastic wrap. Fan the skein out in an oval to expose as many strands of yarn as possible.

③ Starting with the lightest hue, spray the skeins in bursts of color. Alternate the patches of color to create a pattern. When you have painted one side of the skein, flip it over to paint the other side.

④ Wrap the skeins in plastic and steam.

TIP

For less diffused bursts of color, paint a thin layer of thickener on the yarn before applying the color. This will prevent the color spray from traveling and give a more distinct effect. I dilute the thickener with 1 teaspoon of water and apply it to the yarn with a plastic fork. The tines of the fork help to coat the strands of yarn. Don't worry about applying the thickener evenly—it's nearly impossible to do because it is clear and difficult to see.

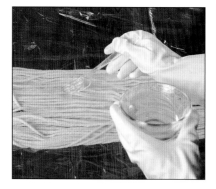

Yarns and Roving Dyed with Spray-Bottle Method

Wool roving spray-dyed with a fine mist, in two colors.

Colors applied in bursts on silk roving.

This yarn was lightly spray-dyed without thickener for an airbrushed effect.

Thickener was painted onto the skein before the dye was applied.

Microwave Casserole Method

Microwave dyeing is a quick and easy way to dye small quantities of protein fiber using acid dyes. It is a great method for dyeing fiber for a small project or for quickly sampling colorways. Use the microwave method to touch up white spots on hand-painted yarns.

The following process reveals a trick for creating a surprisingly lively hand-painted yarn from loosely wound center-pull balls of wool yarn.

Specifications

MATERIALS

- 4 loosely wound center-pull balls of wool yarn, approximately 100 yards (91m) per ball
- 100ml 1% dye stock WashFast solution, Reddish Brown
- 100ml 1% dye stock in two accent colors: WashFast Plum and Chinese Red

TOOLS

- Pyrex casserole dish with cover
- Plastic syringes with long, narrow tips
- Microwave oven

Note: Once a microwave oven is used in dyeing, it should never be used for food preparation, so look for an inexpensive or used model for craft projects.

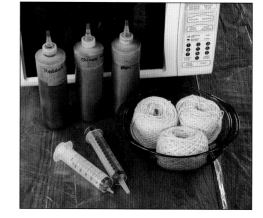

SAFETY

Microwave dyeing transfers dye and acid vapors into the room during the steaming process. Always use ventilation and a vapor mask to avoid inhalation of the fumes. Follow all guidelines for safe dyeing as described in "Safety Essentials" in Chapter 2. Never use dyeing tools or equipment for food preparation.

 TIP

Fiber that has been cooked in a microwave oven becomes extremely hot. Wear oven mitts when handling the dishes. If you need to handle hot fiber, use tongs or a spoon.

Preparation

Presoak the balls of yarn in an acid solution (see Chapter 4) for at least 1 hour to ensure that the solution completely saturates the yarn balls.

Remove the yarn balls from the acid soak and gently squeeze to remove excess water. The yarn should be damp but not dripping wet. Use a small towel to blot excess water before dyeing.

Pour 100ml of the Reddish Brown dye stock into the casserole dish and arrange the balls in the dish.

Inject the Dye and Microwave

Using a plastic syringe, draw approximately 10ml of the Reddish Brown dye solution and inject it into the center of each ball. This will help evenly distribute the main color.

Use a plastic syringe to inject pockets of the accent colors at evenly spaced intervals. Starting with Chinese Red, draw approximately 12ml of dye stock into the syringe. Inject in even increments into the side of each yarn ball. Draw the same amount of the Plum dye stock into the syringe and inject pockets of color in equal amounts in four places near the top of the ball. Use the tip of the syringe to penetrate the yarn ball so that the color reaches the yarn in the center.

CONTINUED ON NEXT PAGE

Place the cover partially over the casserole dish and place it in the microwave. Set the timer for 2 minutes. Allow the yarn to sit for 2 minutes, then turn the balls upside down and inject about 12ml of Plum dye stock in four places at the top of each yarn ball. Then cover the dish and place it in the microwave for another 2 minutes to set the dye.

Note: *Use hot mitts when handling the hot dish; do not attempt to handle the yarn when hot.*

Rinse and Rewind

Allow the balls of yarn to cool completely before rinsing in the sink with warm water and Synthrapol. This step is a good indication of whether the dye has bonded with the fiber. Excessive bleeding in the water means you need to dip the yarn in white vinegar or a mild acid solution and then steam in the microwave for another 2 minutes to set the dye.

Use a towel to press the excess water out of the yarn and place the yarn balls on a flat surface with good air circulation to dry.

When the yarn is partially dry, rewind each ball into a skein. This is the exciting moment when you see the pattern created by the pockets of injected dye. Give the skein another warm rinse to remove any residual dye. If you notice excess dye bleeding at this stage, dip the skeins in vinegar and place them in the microwave for another 2 minutes.

Micro-Method Tips and Variations

Microwave ovens can also be used to create space-dyed yarns. Use a direct pour method to add color to skeins in an oblong Pyrex baking dish. Be careful not to add too much dye. Steam the skeins for 2 minutes, then let them sit for 2 minutes. Turn the skeins to ensure even temperature distribution and then steam for another 2 minutes.

To create solid or semisolid skeins, immerse the skeins in a pot of dye stock containing acid to absorb the dye. Place the color-soaked skeins in a casserole dish and steam as described above.

Use a syringe or squeeze bottle to add a contrasting color to the skeins. Place the dish back in the microwave oven. Set for 2 minutes, remove the dish and rotate the yarn. Place the dish back in the microwave oven and cook for another 2 minutes.

Microwave ovens vary in power, so you'll need to do some sampling to determine the length of time needed to set the dye. Test the colorfastness of the yarn in a warm bath to make sure the dye has completely adhered. You may need to rinse the yarn in vinegar or a mild citric acid solution and steam again. Test the yarn for dye penetration by gently unplying the yarn with your fingers.

Sun-Soaked Skeins

Mason jars filled with yarn and color steep in the sun's warmth for amazing results. The success of solar dyeing depends on your geography. If you live in the tropics, the sun's heat on a hot day may be strong enough to set the dye. If the sun's rays are less intense where you live, you can still use this method to slowly steep skeins or balls of yarn in multiple layers of color, but you will need to steam the Mason jars afterward to ensure a permanent bond.

Create the Colors

In the following demonstration, I create six tertiary colors from three primaries. You can vary this exercise by substituting another set of primary colors or by using preformulated colors.

MATERIALS

- 4 100-yard (91m) balls or skeins
- 4 cups (1,000ml) 1% dye stock WashFast dyes: Sun Yellow 119, Bright Red 351, National Blue 425c

TOOLS

- 1-pint Mason jars (wide-mouth jars work best)
- Plastic syringe for injecting dye
- Plastic fork
- Canning pot with rack and lid

Note: *The yarn must be presoaked in an acid solution for one hour ahead of time (see Chapter 4). If you are working with balls of yarn, use a nylon mesh bag to keep the balls intact during the presoak.*

Create 4 cups (1,000ml) 1% stock solution of each color (see Chapter 5 for instructions on mixing dye stock). Then mix six colors combining the three stock solutions as follows to make 3.5 ounces (100ml) of each new color. Using metric measurements makes it easier to measure small amounts of dye for the blends.

Color 1: 80ml Yellow, 10ml Red, 10ml Blue
Color 2: 30ml Yellow, 40ml Red, 30ml Blue
Color 3: 50ml Yellow, 10ml Red, 40ml Blue
Color 4: 40ml Yellow, 50ml Red, 10ml Blue
Color 5: 50ml Yellow, 20ml Red, 30ml Blue
Color 6: 70ml Yellow, 10ml Red, 20ml Blue

Remove the balls of yarn from the acid presoak and gently squeeze to remove excess water. Pour 50ml of each color into a Mason jar and then add 50ml of water to make 100ml of liquid. Stir to combine dye and water.

The Sun Soak

Place one ball of yarn into each jar. Cover the jar and shake well to distribute the dye color. Then place the jars outdoors on a raised surface in a hot, sunny location. This is the sun-steeping process, which is a little like brewing sun tea!

CONTINUED ON NEXT PAGE

Check the jars periodically. Depending on temperature, you will eventually see that the water in the jar has turned clear and the yarn has absorbed the dye. Now inject a second color into the jar. Select a color that contrasts with each of the jars (for example, choose Color 2 to pair with Color 1 or Color 4 to go with Color 6). Use a syringe to add approximately 50ml of the contrasting color into the jar.

Use a plastic fork to gently lift the yarn, allowing the dye to travel down the side of the jar. Use the syringe to draw some of the dye liquid and inject it into the center of the ball.

Replace the lids on the jars and put them back in their sunny warm spot. Allow them to sit for several hours without moving or disturbing the yarn. This is the second half of the steeping process.

Steam, Rinse, and Wind

If you live in a very hot part of the globe, the sun's heat may be sufficient to create the chemical bond between the yarn and dye. The water should be clear at the end of the process. You can check to see if the dye is color fast by washing one of the balls of yarn in warm water with Synthrapol. If you see any color bleeding, place the remaining jars in the canning pot and steam for 30 minutes.

When the yarn has reached room temperature, place the balls back into the nylon mesh bag and rinse them in a warm bath with Synthrapol. Use a second rinse to remove the detergent suds. Press the yarn inside a towel to remove excess moisture or place the bag with yarn in the washing machine to spin out excess water.

The most exciting part of the process comes when you wind the ball into the skein, to see the marble effect created by the interaction of the two contrasting dyes.

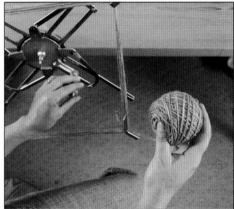

TIP

This project is an interesting way to create six balls of yarn in colors that work well together in the same project. You can repeat this process using any of the WashFast or Cushing primary colors. Select a project that will juxtapose your coordinating yarn colors.

Freckled Roving

Use this process to create a multicolored speckled roving with a slow cooker and an all-in-one dye, such as Gaywool's Bush Blends, which comes with crystals of citric acid mixed in with the grains of dye powder. In this technique, you sprinkle the dye powder directly onto the roving as you place the roving in the pot. Adding just a little water keeps the fiber damp and maintains the freckled effect.

MATERIALS AND TOOLS

- Slow cooker
- Plastic spoons for sprinkling dye
- Gaywool Bush Blends dye in three colors: Ivy, Meadow, and Sugargum
- 10 ounces roving (Bluefaced Leicester used here)

SAFETY

Because this process involves sprinkling dye powder directly onto fiber, you must wear your particle filter mask at all times. Place the caps on the dye powders immediately after using.

PREPARATION

1. Tie the roving into a bundle and soak it in a solution of water and Synthrapol to wet it out for at least half an hour.

2. Remove the roving from the soak and gently extract the excess water. Begin to place the roving in the slow cooker by coiling it in the base of the pot as shown.

Sprinkle the Dye

1 Use a plastic spoon to sprinkle small amounts of each color of dye powder in spots on the first layer of fiber. Be conservative, applying approximately ⅛ teaspoon to each spot.

2 Continue to add roving by winding another tier of the coil into the pot.

3 Sprinkle dye powder on top of the second layer of roving. Then wind another layer of roving and repeat the process. Continue to add small amounts of dye powder to each new layer of roving as you wind the roving coil inside the pot.

4 Add ½ cup water by pouring it around the perimeter of the pot. Place the cover on the pot and cook the roving on the high setting for 1 hour. After the first 20 minutes, check to see that there is some liquid in the bottom of the pot.

Note: *The colors in the bottom half of the pot may run together more than in the top half (since they are sitting in liquid). You can flip the roving over, using tongs, so the colors in the top half also blend.*

5 After one hour, turn off the slow cooker. Let the pot cool before removing the fiber. Rinse the roving and hang to dry.

chapter 9

Dye Cellulose Fibers

This chapter opens the door to the exciting realm of reactive dyes on plant yarns and fiber. Fiber-reactive dyes are the best choice for a wide range of plant fibers. They are easy to use, come in a wide range of colors, and are extremely washfast. The preparation and assists are different than using acid dyes, but many of the same dye application methods can be used.

About Fiber-Reactive Dyes

Since the structure of cellulose fibers prevents them from forming chemical bonds with acid dyes, a different dye class is needed, involving a different chemical process. Reactive dyes work in an *alkaline* environment and form a stronger type of bond with the plant fiber, which makes the colors very washfast. An added advantage is the dye process occurs at room temperature. This is called a *cold pad* dye method. While perfect for plant fibers, these dyes can also be used on silk at room temperature and on wool using a different process involving acid and heat.

Materials and Fiber Preparation

MATERIALS AND TOOLS

The materials used with reactive dyes differ slightly from acid dyes. Here are the materials to have on hand when using fiber-reactive dyes:

- Synthrapol
- Salt
- Soda ash (sodium carbonate)
- Urea (suggested for hand-painting)
- Sodium alginate (dye thickener, optional for hand-painting)

Note: *Use the same tools that are used for acid dyeing. Once tools are used for dyeing, they should never be used for food preparation.*

SAFETY

When using reactive dyes, follow the same safety precautions that apply to using acid dyes (see Chapter 2). Always wear a particle mask when mixing dye powder. Never eat or prepare food when working with dye. Alkaline solutions are caustic and will sting on contact with your skin. Wear long rubber gloves to protect your hands and arms and wear safety glasses to protect your eyes from splashes.

Prepare Fiber for Dyeing

Plant fibers need a scouring process to prepare them for dyeing.

1 Prepare a hot scour soak by adding boiling water to a sink half full of hot tap water.

2 Add ½ teaspoon Synthrapol and ½ teaspoon soda ash.

3 Submerge the yarn or fiber and soak for 1 hour.

4 Rinse the skeins thoroughly in warm water after scouring.

This process can be done in advance of dyeing. If you plan to dye a large quantity of fiber, it can be done in a washing machine.

TIP

Alkaline Presoak for Direct Application Methods

When using either of the direct application methods described in this chapter, soak the fibers in an alkaline presoak for 15 minutes just before dyeing. The presence of alkalinity in the fiber is needed for the dye bond to happen when you paint (or pour) on the dye.

The alkaline soak contains 9 tablespoons (80g) of soda ash in 1 gallon (4L) of warm water. The soak is caustic, so take care when adding and removing fibers. Make the soak in a plastic bucket with a lid so it can be stored and reused for future projects.

Immersion-Dye Cotton Yarn

Soft, fluffy cotton skeins are beautiful dyed in pastel shades. Cotton requires a thorough hot scour in preparation for dyeing. To achieve deep colors when immersion dyeing with MX reactive dye, it is important to use the proper amount of salt and the correct amount of soda ash.

Prepare Fiber for Dyeing

MATERIALS AND TOOLS

- 4 four-ounce skeins (454g) unmercerized cotton yarn
- PRO MX Dye (example uses Bordeaux #319)
- Synthrapol
- Soda ash
- Salt
- 40-quart stainless steel pot
- Measuring cup and spoons
- Long-handled spoon for stirring

1 Scour the skeins as described on page 159.

2 Mix a dye stock for a pale color value by adding 1 gram of dye powder to 2 cups (500ml) water. Stir thoroughly.

The Reactive Dye Bath

PART ONE

The goal of the first part of a reactive dye bath is to encourage the dye to penetrate the fiber evenly for a level result. This step does not actually bond the dye to the fiber. Salt is used to charge the dye bath. It coaxes the dye out of the water and onto the fiber. The amount of salt depends on the depth of color.

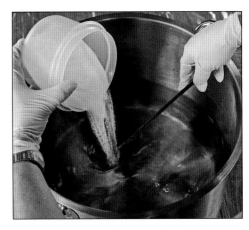

1 For a pale depth of shade, add 1 pound (454g) of salt to 2½ gallons (10L) of room temperature water and stir until the salt dissolves completely. Then add the dye stock and stir.

2 Add the skeins to the dye bath and swish them back and forth gently for 5 minutes to distribute the dye evenly on the yarn.

3 Lift the skeins, stir the pot, put the skeins back in the pot, and swish continuously for another 10 minutes. The more you manipulate the skeins, the more even your results will be.

PART TWO

The second part of the dye bath triggers the reactive process. The addition of soda ash raises the alkalinity and fixes the dye to the fiber.

1 Make a soda ash solution by dissolving 5 tablespoons (45g) of soda ash in 2 cups (500ml) of warm water.

2 Remove the skeins from the pot and add the soda ash solution.

3 Stir thoroughly and place the skeins back into the pot.

4 Swish the skeins continuously in the dye bath for the first 5 minutes as the bonding process takes place. Then continue to manipulate the skeins every 5 minutes for the next hour to ensure an even bond.

CONTINUED ON NEXT PAGE

5 Forty minutes into this process, you will have an idea of how much dye will be left over in the bath. There will be some dye left in the pot, due to the nature of reactive dyes. At the end of 1 hour, the process is complete.

Note: A reactive dye bath will have a very high pH and must be neutralized before disposal. To neutralize the bath, add vinegar, one tablespoon at a time. Check the pH after adding each tablespoon. When you have neutralized the bath, you can pour it down the drain with lots of water.

6 Fibers dyed with reactive dyes require serious rinsing. Fill a sink with room temperature water and rinse the skeins. Repeat this process three times or until the yarn stops bleeding color. A final hot water rinse is then needed in 140°F water with Synthrapol added.

7 Cotton dries slowly. Spin the water out of the skeins to speed the drying time and hang the skeins to dry.

Bamboo fiber draws dye like a wick, making it exciting to use in hand-paint (and dip-dye) methods. Hand-painting with reactive dyes is quite similar to the process of hand-painting with acid dyes. While many of the steps are the same, there are differences in materials and procedures. Reactive dyes cure at room temperature. This project shows painting eight 2-ounce skeins of bamboo yarn. I use varying combinations and proportions of five colors to shift the emphasis from one hue to another. The Fibonacci number series 3, 5, 8 determines the color proportions.

Prepare Fiber for Dyeing

MATERIALS

- 8 two-ounce skeins (454g) bamboo yarn
- PRO MX Reactive Dyes in five colors: Chartreuse 706, Loden 7157, Stormy Grey 6160, Dusty Purple 805, and Wisteria 820
- Synthrapol
- Soda ash
- Urea
- Sodium alginate dye thickener (optional)
- Plastic wrap

TOOLS

- Measuring cups and spoons
- 5-cup containers for holding dye
- 5 one-inch foam brushes
- Coffee filter papers

SAFETY

Be sure to follow the safety guidelines in Chapter 2. Wear a particle mask when mixing dye solutions. Be careful when removing skeins from an alkaline soak, as this solution is caustic.

CONTINUED ON NEXT PAGE

Scour the yarn following the process described on page 159. Create an alkaline solution soak as described at the beginning of this chapter.

The presence of alkalinity is needed for the painted dyes to bond with the fiber during the curing process. The presoak raises the pH of the fiber so it can accept the dye. Soak the skeins for 15 minutes before painting.

Next you will mix the dye solutions by adding urea water to the dye powder. Urea acts as a humectant and keeps the fibers moist long enough for the curing to take place.

MAKE THE DYE SOLUTIONS

1. Make the urea water by adding 9 tablespoons (100g) of urea to 1 quart (1L) of warm water. You will use 1 cup (250ml) of urea water for each of the dyes, so be sure to mix it all at once.

2. Use the urea water to create the dye solutions. For a paler value, mix 1g of dye powder with 1 cup (250ml) of urea water for a medium value. For a deeper value, use 5g of dye.

TIP

Use coffee filter papers to help compose your color palette. Experiment with color order by placing colors side by side in different combinations and proportions using any number of the five colors. Try several variations on paper before painting the skeins.

Paint the Skeins

1 Remove the skeins from the alkaline soak just prior to painting so that they will remain damp.

2 Gently press out excess water and place each skein on a sheet of plastic wrap.

3 Mark your color sequence on the plastic, using a ruler. For the Fibonacci number series, use a pen to mark intervals of 3, 5, and 8 inches.

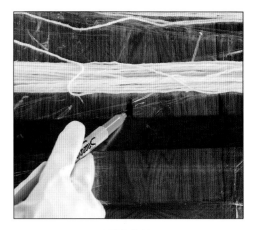

4 Paint the skeins using foam brushes, starting with the lightest color. Work your way around the skein, taking care not to contaminate your brush where two colors meet. Try different combinations. On one skein, use the brightest color for the shortest section, then work your way through the progression. Reverse the sequence on another skein, using the darkest color for the shortest band in the color repeat.

Note: In this series, I started by painting the first skein with Chartreuse, Stormy Grey, and Dusty Purple in 3-, 5-, and 8-inch segments, respectively, working my way around the skein. In another skein, I used the same proportions, but substituted the colors Wisteria, Dusty Purple, and Loden. For one skein, I mixed another color, Brick, and sampled that with Dusty Purple and Stormy Grey.

5 Wipe any excess dye and wrap each skein in plastic.

6 Set the skeins on a tray to cure the dye. It takes at least 4 hours for this to happen. The room temperature must be at least 70°F for success. If you are dyeing dark colors, up to 24 hours may be needed. After the yarn has cured, follow the rinsing procedure as described for the cotton immersion process.

Note: Painting 8 skeins will use most of the dye. Leftover reactive dyes mixed with urea water can be stored in tightly closed bottles and used within 5 days of mixing.

Tencel has the highest luster of the plant fibers used in this chapter. Its incredible sheen reflects colors in a spectacular way. As with other lustrous fibers, you need to use stronger dye stocks to achieve deeper values. Use the spontaneity of randomly pouring dye directly onto the fiber to create exciting rovings for hand spinning. Limiting your colors to three and pouring dye conservatively will help avoid muddy hues.

MATERIALS

- 4 one-ounce hanks of Tencel roving
- PRO MX Reactive Dyes in two colors (I used Brick 520 and Bordeaux 319)
- Synthrapol
- Soda ash
- Urea
- Dye thickener (optional)

TOOLS

- Measuring cups and spoons
- Beakers for pouring dye
- Gallon-size locking seal plastic bags
- Baster or syringe for adding touches of color

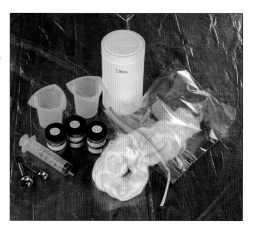

PREPARATION

Follow the same preparation steps used in dyeing the bamboo yarn. Scour the roving and soak in an alkaline solution for 15 minutes before dyeing. Tie the roving in small bundles to keep it intact during the presoak.

COLOR POUR

Place a damp hank of roving inside a locking seal plastic bag by snaking the fiber back and forth. Expose as much fiber surface area as possible.

Note: *You can dye each 1-ounce hank of roving in its own bag, using different colors in varying patterns and proportions. You will have 4 ounces of color-themed roving to incorporate in one small project.*

Use the beaker to pour the colors in spots directly onto the fiber. Gently massage the roving so the dye penetrates the hank. Add dye to cover any white spots. Pour small amounts of color at a time. I used Bordeaux as the overall color with splashes of Brick as an accent color.

Use a baster or syringe to apply random dashes of color. A syringe will give you the most control in applying small amounts of dye. Be conservative—adding excessive amounts will cause colors to lose their definition and run together. When you have finished, seal the bag and cure for 24 hours. Follow the rinsing instructions provided earlier in this chapter and hang the roving to dry.

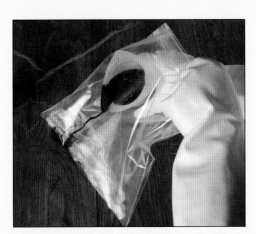

chapter 10

Color on Color: The Artful Overdye

Overdyeing is the process of transforming dyed yarns or naturally colored fibers by dyeing over the original color. Dyes are a transparent medium. Adding a layer of color over another color creates a rich and complex new color. You can use any of the methods described in the preceding chapters to overdye for solid-color or variegated yarns.

When overdyeing solid colors to form new solid colors, you will use the color-blending concepts discussed in Chapter 5. Color-on-color opens the door for textural effects and imaginative palettes when using hand-paint techniques. Overdyeing naturally colored fibers creates colors with depth and variations of shade.

Use overdye to create coordinating companion yarns to pair with solid colors. This process can also salvage a dye pot disaster or transform an ugly duckling yarn into something beautiful.

Overdye Natural-Colored Fibers

Natural fibers come in a wide range of colors. Wool colors range from ecru to latte, chestnut brown, musket gray, and silver. Alpaca fiber comes in shades of fawn, cinnamon, buff, and black. Even silk fibers range from a soft champagne to a deep honey tone. Use immersion or direct application methods to transform fibers with a natural color base into richly colored yarns.

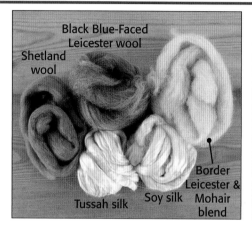

Shetland wool

Black Blue-Faced Leicester wool

Tussah silk

Soy silk

Border Leicester & Mohair blend

CHARACTERISTICS OF OVERDYED NATURAL-COLORED FIBERS

Dyeing naturally colored fibers results in rich, subdued tones. Colors that might appear bright or garish on white fibers appear deep and sophisticated on naturally colored fibers. Because dye is a transparent medium, the undertone of the fiber's natural shade comes through.

Naturally colored fibers are often composed of fibers in a range of shades. Look closely at the skein of yarn (a), a blend of colored wool and alpaca fibers comprised of gray, brown, silver, and ecru strands. Each of the naturally colored strands accepts dye differently, resulting in the heather color shown in (b).

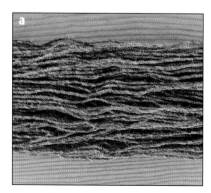

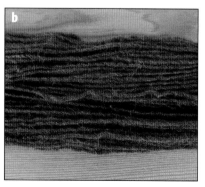

The skeins were immersion dyed to let the yarn's original character and texture show.

Keeping some of the natural silver-beige of the wool and mohair in this hand-painted roving adds another dimension when spun into yarn.

CONTINUED ON NEXT PAGE

IMMERSION DYE BATH ON NATURAL COLORS

To dye a naturally colored yarn or roving a solid or semisolid color, follow the steps for immersion dyeing in Chapter 6. Use pale values at first (you can always deepen a color by dyeing again), working with dye stock in strengths of 0.1% or 0.5%. Remember, a 0.1% dye solution is created using 1g of dye to 1,000ml of water. Make a 0.5% dye stock by adding 5g of dye powder to 1,000ml of water. This will keep the yarn or fiber from becoming too dark, which would obscure the natural shading.

LOW WATER TECHNIQUE

Combine several shades of naturally colored wool or other animal fiber in a low-water immersion dye bath. Each fiber will take the dye differently. When carded and spun together, the fibers will make a unique semisolid yarn with variations in texture and shade.

HAND-PAINT ON NATURAL COLORS

When hand-painting on naturally colored yarn or roving, experiment by allowing some of the fiber's natural color to remain undyed. In a roving, the fiber's natural color diffuses the painted colors for a soft effect. In a hand-painted skein, showing some of the yarn's original natural color becomes a design feature.

Overdye Commercial Yarns

You can overdye to transform commercial yarns by adding layers of color. The following examples show how to create both semisolid and patterned yarns by dyeing on top of a base color. Use these methods to dye interesting companion yarns, letting the base color be the unifying theme.

Search your yarn stash for "ugly ducklings," or find them inexpensively in the bargain bin at the yarn store—the colors no one liked! Use them to experiment with overdyeing.

TRANSFORM SOLID COLORS

To alter a solid color, select an analogous color that contrasts with the original color of the yarn. Mix a 0.1% stock solution of the contrasting color and create an immersion dye bath for the yarn, following the steps in Chapter 6 (consult the formula in Chapter 5 for calculating the amount of dye needed for the total weight of fiber). In the example shown to the right, I overdyed a pale gold yarn with a contrasting color, WashFast Mahogany 508.

Use the spray-paint method described in Chapter 8 to subdue bright colors or add dimensional color. In the example on the right, I spray-dyed a 0.1% solution of WashFast Mahogany 508 over the same gold yarn to create a streaky effect.

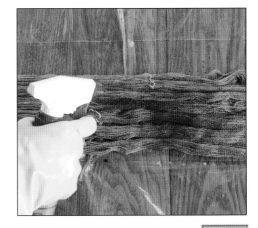

CONTINUED ON NEXT PAGE

HAND-PAINT COMMERCIAL-DYED YARN

Hand-paint techniques create interesting results on solid colors. Here are several variations on the same turquoise-colored yarn with yellow and green applied. The example on the right was dip-dyed in long segments of yellow and green. On the left I painted with thickened yellow and green dyes over the turquoise base using foam brushes and short strokes.

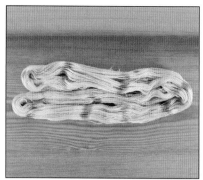

TWIST-RESIST TECHNIQUE

The "twist resist" technique quickly transforms a solid-dye yarn into a hand-painted one. Place a tightly twisted skein in an acid presoak for 30 minutes. Wring out excess water but do not untwist the skein. Thicken ¼ cup of a contrasting dye solution and pour the thickened solution in a Styrofoam tray or shallow pan.

Roll the damp, twisted skein lightly in the thickened dye. The outer bumps in the skein will pick up the dye, while the twisted inner sections will retain the original color. The spiral wrap of the skein acts as a resist, creating a yarn with a tie-dye pattern. Wrap the skein in plastic and steam to set the dye.

The heather technique mimics the appearance of a yarn dyed in the wool. Yarn manufacturers sometimes combine multiple colors of dyed fibers to create a tweed effect in a finished yarn. You can simulate that look by dyeing a yarn a solid base color then applying flecks of several closely related contrasting colors. Flashes of multiple colors add depth to an almost solid-looking yarn.

How to Heather

① The first step is to dye the yarn a base color. Prepare an acid dye bath using a 0.1% dye stock, following the steps in Chapter 6. I used WashFast Golden Pear 120. Allow the skeins to soak in the acid dye bath without heat until they have absorbed the color and the water is clear. This will happen over a few hours, or you can let the skeins sit overnight. The yarn absorbs the dye, but the chemical bond has not yet taken place in the absence of heat.

② Press the water out of the skeins and place them on plastic wrap. Fan out the yarn to expose as many strands as possible.

③ Mix 1 cup (250ml) of each contrasting color dye solution at a strength of 1%. I used WashFast Herb Green 709, Country Green 710, Golden Pear 120 (at a deeper value of the original color), and Gold Yellow 199c.

④ Add 4 tablespoons (80ml) of Superclear dye thickener to each solution.

CONTINUED ON NEXT PAGE

5 Use a 10ml plastic syringe to apply dots of color. Work in a pattern, so each color will be evenly distributed throughout the yarn.

6 Drizzle the color in droplets, rather than spraying it onto the yarn. The thickener will help maintain the pin-prick color effect rather than allowing the drops of dye to bleed and disappear.

7 Allow the skein to sit for 10 minutes, then turn the skeins to paint the other side. After letting the skeins sit for another 10 minutes, wrap them in plastic to steam. Follow the guidelines for steaming yarn skeins (described on pages 107–108).

This technique creates a semisolid appearance with multiple colors applied over a base color using the spray paint method described in Chapter 8. Spraying color over color adds depth and subtle shading to yarn without creating a definitive color pattern.

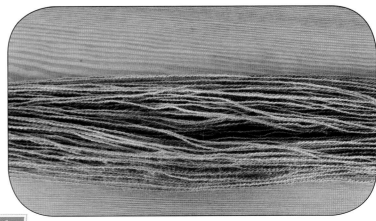

Spray Skeins for an Atmospheric Effect

1 As with the previous method, you begin by dyeing the yarn a solid base color in a pale value. In the example, I start with an acid dye bath of WashFast Slate Blue 441 in a 0.1% strength of solution. Let the skeins soak in a pot of acid dye stock until the yarn has absorbed all the dye.

2 Remove the skeins from the dye soak and press out excess water. This method works best if the skeins are slightly damp. Fan the skeins open on a sheet of plastic wrap.

3 Mix 1 cup (250ml) of two dye solutions in deeper colors (a 0.1% strength of solution). You can even use a deeper shade of the original base color. For a yarn to read as a semisolid, select two colors close in hue to the base color. I used WashFast Turquoise 478 and a 1% solution of the original color, Slate Blue.

4 Place the cooled solutions in spray bottles.

CONTINUED ON NEXT PAGE

5 Wearing a safety mask, lightly spray the first color over the surface of the skein, evenly covering with a fine mist while retaining the base color background. Allow the first color to dry for several minutes before applying the second color.

6 Apply the second color in the same fashion, spreading a fine mist over the surface of the skein. Allow several minutes for this color to set. Then turn the skein to spray the reverse side using both colors.

7 Wrap the skeins in plastic wrap and steam, following the steps in Chapter 8.

Skeins of yarn dyed with the atmospheric spray-paint method and a sock knit from them.

A cone of turquoise yarn with overdyed skeins.

chapter 11

Spin and Knit with Hand-Dyed Fiber

Projects created from hand-dyed fibers are personalized and one of a kind. The transformation from painted roving or hand-dyed skeins to exuberant stitches in colorways of your own design is magic—the reward for your work in the dye studio.

This chapter provides some suggestions for using hand-dyed fiber in a variety of techniques. When planning a project, consider the special characteristics of hand-dyed fibers and how to make the most of them.

Spin with Hand-Painted Roving

The best part about spinning yarn from hand-painted roving is that it gives you room to take your creativity a step further before you take the final step: knitting a garment. Spinners have the luxury of deciding how to use painted fibers to best enhance color features. The realm of possibilities for further color combinations is vast—and several excellent books are devoted to that topic (see the bibliography). Here are some ideas for extending color creativity with a spindle.

Variegated Roving

A hand-painted roving holds a world of possibilities. The most obvious and straightforward option is to simply spin the roving as it is presented, but there are really many paths. Spinning toward a goal—a pair of mittens or socks or a lace scarf—will help guide your choices. Or you can simply spin and see what happens.

SPIN TO KEEP COLORS INTACT

Consider how quickly you want to see color shifts in the yarn. If your roving has long bands of color and a long repeat, you could spin for yards before seeing a shift in hue, which makes it easy to spin your own self-striping yarn. Split your roving into pencil-thin strips (a) and draft the strips into wispy strands. Doing so gets it closer in diameter to the finished yarn (b) and gives you a sense of how long before a color change occurs. The thinner the roving, the faster the color changes will be.

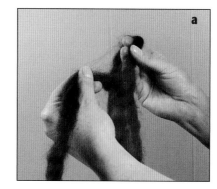
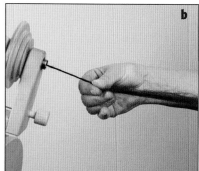

If your goal is to create a striping yarn, you need to do some planning. Because striping yarns have long stretches of color, you do not necessarily want to draft the roving into pencil-thin strips. But you would want to keep the colors intact in the final yarn. It is possible to carefully divide a painted roving into even sections that, when spun on separate bobbins and then plied together, more or less match up colorwise.

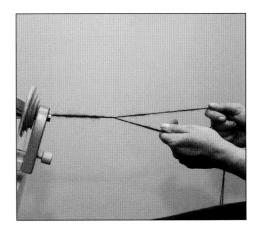

Another option is to spin a balanced single that needs no plying. A single ply yarn is not as strong as a two ply, so you may not want to spin sock yarn in this way. A third possibility is to ply the variegated single with a thin solid color thread, which would be inconspicuous in the final plied yarn.

Navajo plying is a good solution for producing a sturdy, three-ply yarn from just a single strand. It has the added advantage of keeping gorgeous hand-painted colors intact. This technique involves chaining the yarn through a loop, much like a chain stitch in crochet, as you treadle the wheel.

CONTINUED ON NEXT PAGE

SPIN TO DISTRIBUTE COLOR

Variegated roving can yield beautiful yarns with an entirely different effect. The alternative to spinning to maintain pure colors is to spin so that there is maximum interaction between colors. These techniques create more opportunities for juxtaposed colors and distribute the colors a bit more uniformly throughout the yarn.

Strip a painted roving into pencil-thin strips in 30-inch lengths. Realign the strips so the colors do not match up. Predraft the strands of roving together and spin them as one. There will be multiple colors spun together throughout the yarn. A yarn spun this way becomes even more interesting when plied onto itself.

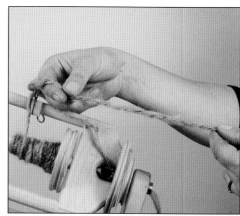

Random Dyed Roving

Roving dyed in one of the freestyle methods has a heather appearance. Colors become less distinct in the process of drafting the fibers. The overall effect is a subdued semisolid yarn with incidental color accents.

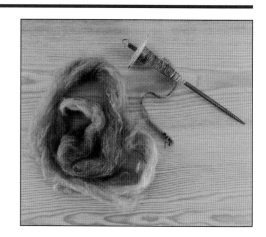

TIP

Sometimes spinners are disappointed when spinning a beautifully dyed roving, only to see the colors become muddy. This often occurs when color complements are drafted together to form a dull color (for example, a roving dyed with red and green side by side might become brown as the red and green fibers are drafted together). To avoid muddy blends, you can separate a roving by breaking into its component colors and then spin each color one at a time, making quick transitions when changing colors. The transitions between colors will be more abrupt, but you will lose the muddy effect for stretches of yarn where complementary colors merge.

Yarns from Hand-Dyed Roving

This lace-weight single was spun from a hand-painted blend of cashmere and tussah silk.

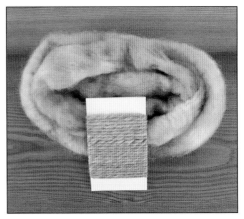

Playful flecks of color dance on a white backdrop in this Cormo wool yarn.

Allowing the natural colors of Border Leicester and mohair fibers to show in the hand-painted roving gives this yarn an earthy color and texture.

Navajo plying keeps exuberant complementary colors intact.

Dyed-in-the-Wool Works

Locks that are dyed in the wool hold many possibilities for combined colors. Simple processing with cards or combs can yield dramatic effects.

FLICK CARD LOCKS

When long, curly locks are dyed in a rainbow bath, quite often individual locks will have lovely multicolor gradations. A flick card is a tool resembling a slicker dog brush that is used to lightly brush open the ends of fiber staples with a flick of the wrist. Flicking wool locks open and spinning directly from the lock is a minimal preparation that maintains the color integrity of each individual lock. The process is slow since you must flick each lock individually, but the final result is worth the effort.

Place the flicked locks in a shoe box and separate the layers with tissue paper. Spin them one lock at a time, drafting as you go.

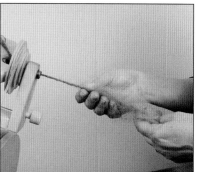

HAND CARD MULTICOLOR ROLAGS

Blending colored locks of wool on hand cards creates beautiful rolags. A *rolag* is a carded fiber preparation. Fibers are brushed open to form a sheet, then rolled into a tube for spinning. To form a multicolor rolag, load the card cloth from left to right, alternating the color of wool staples. When you brush the locks to open the fibers, the colors fan together. Spin them into a colorful, lofty woolen yarn.

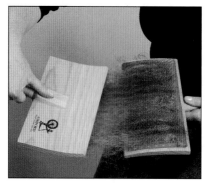

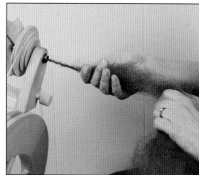

A drum carder is a useful tool for combining multicolored and solid-dyed fibers. You can use a drum carder in several ways to blend hand-dyed fiber. For instance, you can combine three different solid-dyed rovings to create a tricolor batt. Feed three thin stripes of color onto the drum at once.

Colors can also be carded in layers. Feed one color onto the drum at a time in thin sheets of color. By stacking the colors on top of each other, all colors are present at once when you spin from the batt.

 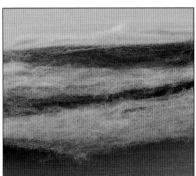

Drum carding small amounts of accent fibers adds an exciting dimension to hand-dyed, hand-spun yarn. Fold touches of Angelina, a sparkling nylon novelty fiber available in many colors, into the wool as you card the batt. Just a little sparkle goes a long way.

 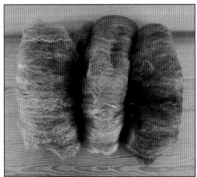

Knit with Hand-Dyed Yarns

The artistry of hand-dyed yarn enhances any knitting project. Hand-dyed yarns have their own character. Pairing them thoughtfully with the appropriate project shows the yarn and the knitting to its best advantage. Since dye baths are one-of-a-kind, always be sure you have enough dyed yarn for your planned project.

Solid and Semisolid Color Yarns

Solid and semisolid color yarns are typically used when the emphasis is on stitch pattern. Where hand-painted yarns can detract from elaborate cable work, the subtle variations of shade in hand-dyed solids adds depth and character. The unmistakable mark of the dyer's hand sets hand-dyed solids apart from commercially dyed yarns.

Semisolid yarns are more broken in color, without an overall color pattern. Their mottled appearance adds dimensional color to the knitted swatch without detracting from the pattern.

Fair Isle stitches in saturated hand-dyed hues.

Overdyed yarn lends texture to twisted cables.

Hand-dyed colors woven in entrelac stitch.

TIP

There tends to be some unevenness to solidly dyed skeins. This may not matter in a small project like a hat, but it could affect the appearance of a sweater. To even out the appearance of the yarn, knit from alternating skeins of the same color. This will break up any areas within a skein where the dye streaked or blotched.

Knit with Hand-Painted Yarns

The excitement of knitting with hand-painted yarn comes from watching colors play out in a stitch pattern. When you have dyed colorways for your own projects, you have the advantage of tailoring a color pattern to the design. Length of colors in hand-painted yarn plays a big role in determining the outcome. Colors can be in stripes or dashes or can have an overall mottled effect. Select the stitch that enhances your color designs.

Short bands of color in a repeating pattern (a) enlivens basic stockinette stitches. In analogous colors, the effect is harmonious and balanced.

Longer bands of color make spirals or striping patterns in stockinette (b). Skeins of big circumference make larger stripes possible.

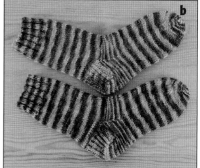

TIP

Chapter 7 briefly discusses pooling, which is what happens when colors in a hand-painted skein stack up in unanticipated ways, creating their own patterns. If you find this feature of hand-painted yarn distracting, there are a few things you can do:

- Try knitting from alternate skeins as described earlier in this chapter. This will break up any color pattern and create a knitted piece with all-over color.
- Try changing your gauge. Increasing or decreasing the number of stitches per inch will affect the positioning of colors. This may mean modifying your choice of project ultimately, if you are dissatisfied with the way the colors work at a given gauge and are unable to change gauge.
- Try different stitch patterns. Any stitch pattern with movement (such as slip-stitch and diagonal lace) will somewhat mitigate the self-patterning of a yarn that pools.

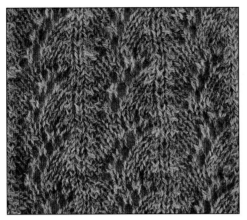

Lace patterns break up the horizontal striations of hand-paints and create movement in color.

Moss stitch becomes multidimensional in this spray-painted color skein.

Solid and hand-painted skeins used in conjunction for a windowpane effect.

Skeins of dappled, sun-soaked skeins form mitered squares of color.

Color Themes for Hand-Dyed Palettes

It is helpful to think of colors thematically when designing hand-dye palettes. This chapter shows how thematic concepts can inspire colorways. The yarns and fibers shown were dyed using many of the methods described in this book.

The changing colors of the seasons on my New England farm inspired the palettes shown.

Hand-painted skeins reflect the colors of Indian summer.

Autumn leaves inspire hand-painted skeins using Cushing Dyes: Brown Rust and Mahogany.

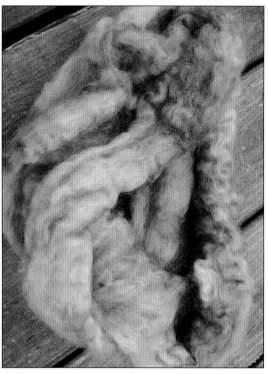

The colors of a winter sky. Gaywool Dyes: Violet, Logwood, Silver Birch.

Painted skeins inspired by early spring (dyed using Atmospheric Effects method, Chapter 10).

Hand-painted tencel skein in the colors of summer fields and skies.

Kettle-dyed skeins reflect the colors of woodlands and meadows.

Lavender harvest (immersion-dyed with Cushing Silver Gray).

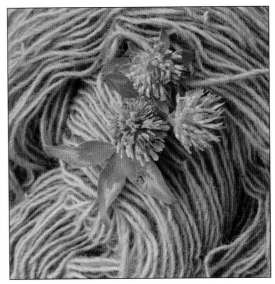

A field of clover.

Magnolia blossoms (immersion-dyed with WashFast Pink Sand).

Tiger lily-inspired skeins.

CONTINUED ON NEXT PAGE

Botanically inspired hand-painted skeins.

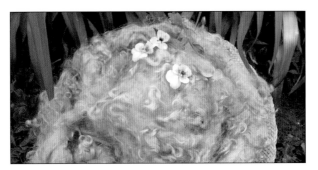

Wool locks dyed using leftover dye baths.

Woodland skeins dyed using the direct pour low-level immersion technique.

Cranberry skeins dyed using the microwave method.

Silk roving in the colors of spices—immersion dyed.

Cormo wool and silk in the colors of sweet potato & yams (dyed in low-water immersion method, Cushing Golden Brown, Egyptian Red, Brown Rust).

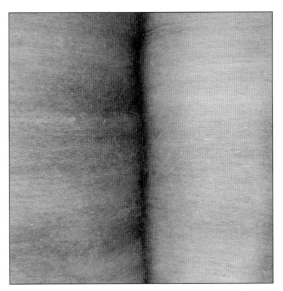

Ginger-colored batts. (Solid-dyed roving colors blended on drum carder with Angelina fiber.)

Glossary of Hand-Dyeing Terms

Acid dye   A class of dyes that require an acid to bond with fiber. Used on protein fibers.

Alkaline   The upper range (8–14) on the pH scale.

Analogous colors   Three colors adjacent to one another on a color wheel.

Angora   The fiber from an Angora rabbit; *OR* a species of goat that produces mohair.

Batt   A sheet of fiber that has been drum-carded to align the fibers.

Camelid   Fiber-producing mammals belonging to the family Camelidae, including llamas, alpacas, camels, vicunas, and guanacos.

Cellulose   A carbohydrate polymer that is the main substance found in plant fibers.

Citric acid   A weak, food-grade acid commonly used in dyeing protein fibers with acid dyes.

Cold pad dyeing   The dyeing process using fiber-reactive dyes at room temperature and curing the fibers wrapped in plastic.

Complementary colors   Colors that lie directly opposite each other on a color wheel.

Dehair   To remove coarse guard hairs from fibers such as llama and alpaca.

Depth of shade   Color value determined by the amount of dye to dry weight of fiber.

Drafting   The process of pulling out fibers to a certain thickness for handspinning.

Dye assist   Material used in dyeing to assist a chemical bond between dye molecules and fiber. Citric acid is an acid dye assist. Soda ash is the dye assist for reactive dyes.

Dye in the grease   To dye unwashed wool.

Dye in the wool   To dye wool in its natural lock formation (before combing or spinning).

Dye liquor   The liquid in a dye bath which includes dye, water, leveling agents, and assists.

Dye stock   A solution made by combining water and dye powder. (Also referred to as dye solution.)

Dye strike   The process of liquid dye attaching to fiber.

Exhaust   The process of dye bonding with fiber to where dye is no longer present in a dye bath.

Felting   The process of wool (or other protein fibers) becoming matted by the locking of scales on the surface of the fiber. Soap, agitation, and a change in temperature cause felting.

Fiber-reactive dye   The class of dye that reacts with cellulose fiber molecules (plant).

Fibonacci numbers   A numerical sequence found in nature that creates pleasing proportions. The next number in a sequence is the sum of the two preceding numbers.

Glauber salt   Sodium sulfate. Used in place of common table salt.

Guar gum   A dye thickener used in hand-painting with acid dyes.

Hue   The name of a color found on the color wheel.

Keratin   The protein substance that forms wool, hair, and other animal fibers.

Lanolin   The naturally occurring greasy substance on sheep's wool.

Leveling agent   A material such as salt used to assist in the even penetration of dye.

Locks   The natural structure of a bunch of wool (or mohair). A fleece separated will come apart in locks (also called *staples*) of wool.

Mohair   The lustrous fiber produced by Angora goats.

Mordant   A material used in natural dyeing to enable the dye stuff to bond with fiber. Alum is the safest mordant used in natural dyeing.

Optical mixing   The visual blending that happens when two colors appear to combine to form a new color when seen from a distance.

Primary colors   The pure colors red, blue, and yellow, from which all other colors are created.

Qiviut   The soft down of the musk ox.

Resist   A compression of fibers using plastic tape, string, stitches, or elastic bands to create pattern in conjunction with dyeing in a process known as tie-dyeing or Shibori.

Rolag   A roll of carded fibers created by hand-carding in preparation for spinning.

Roving   A continuous strand of carded fibers for handspinning. The arrangement of fibers is criss-crossed and random for woolen-style spinning.

Saturation   A color's brightness or clarity.

Scour   To wash raw fleece in preparation for dyeing; *OR* to wash fiber in hot water to remove dirt, grease, sizing, and processing residues before dyeing.

Secondary colors   The colors formed by combining equal parts of two primary colors: orange, green, and purple.

Shades   Darker values of hue created by adding black.

Shibori   The Japanese art of dyeing to create patterns by using resists.

Soda ash   Sodium carbonate; the chemical assist used in reactive dyeing. Soda ash raises the pH of a dye bath.

Sodium alginate   A dye thickener used with fiber-reactive dyes.

Split complement   On the color wheel, the two colors on either side of a color's complement.

Superwash   A process for treating wool fibers to prevent shrinking and felting.

Synthrapol   A pH-neutral surfactant used in wetting out and scouring fibers.

Tertiary colors   Color blends created from any combination of primary colors.

Tints   Lighter color values created by using less dye in a dye stock solution.

Top   A handspinning fiber preparation created by combing fibers into a parallel arrangement while removing shorter fibers; for worsted-style spinning.

Urea   A synthetic nitrogen compound used as a humectant in direct dye applications with fiber-reactive dyes.

Value   The lightness or darkness of a color.

Weight of goods   The dry weight of yarn or fiber before dyeing, used to determine the amount of dye materials needed.

Wet out   To soak fibers in a bath with a surfactant such as Synthrapol prior to dyeing, to enable dyes to penetrate the surface of the fiber more readily.

Appendix

RESOURCES FOR THIS BOOK

DYES AND DYE STUDIO SUPPLIES

Dharma Trading Co.
San Rafael, CA
www.dharmatrading.com

PRO Chemical & Dye
Somerset, MA
www.prochemical.com

YARNS AND FIBERS

Ashland Bay Trading Company
Clackamas, OR
www.ashlandbay.com

Foxfire Fiber & Designs
Shelburne, MA
www.foxfirefiber.com

Henry's Attic
Monroe, NY
www.henrysattic.com

Keldaby Farm
Colrain, MA
www.keldaby.com

Louet North America
www.louet.com

Treenway Silks
Salt Spring Island, British Columbia
www.treenwaysilks.com

Webs
Northampton, MA
www.yarn.com

SOCK BLANKS AND SCARF BLANKS

Dharma Trading Company
San Rafael, CA
www.dharmatrading.com

Machine Knitting to Dye For
San Francisco, CA
www.machineknittingtodyefor.com

Plymouth Yarn
Briston, PA
www.plymouthyarn.com

Knit Picks
www.knitpicks.com

ONLINE RESOURCES

A list of helpful reference websites and discussion groups related to dyeing.

Fibre Arts Online www.fibreartsonline.com
Handweavers Guild of America www.weavespindye.org
Ravelry: A Knit and Crochet Community
www.ravelry.com
Textile Link www.textilelinks.com

Yahoo Groups www.groups.yahoo.com
(There are several Yahoo Groups dedicated
to the topic of dyeing. DyeHappy is the largest.)

FESTIVALS, INSTRUCTIONAL SEMINARS, AND RETREATS

MAJOR FIBER/SHEEP AND WOOL FESTIVALS

One of the best ways to buy fibers is directly from producers. Many fiber festivals also offer workshops on dyeing. Programs and teachers vary from year to year, so check the websites for up-to-date information.

Black Sheep Gathering (June)
Eugene, OR
www.blacksheepgathering.org

Connecticut Sheep, Wool and Fiber Festival (April)
Rockville, CT
www.ctsheep.org

Dixon Lambtown USA (July)
Dixon, CA
www.lambtown.com

Estes Park Wool Market (June)
Estes Park, CO

Maine Fiber Frolic (June)
Windsor, ME
www.fiberfrolic.com

Maryland Sheep and Wool Festival (May)
Baltimore, MD
www.sheepandwoolfestival.org

Massachusetts Sheep and Wool Festival (May)
Cummington, MA
www.masheepwool.org

Michigan Fiber Festival (August)
Allegan, MI
www.michiganfiberfestival.info

New Hampshire Sheep and Wool Festival (May)
Contoocook, NH
www.nhswga.com

New York State Sheep and Wool Festival (October)
Rhinebeck, NY
www.sheepandwool.com

Vermont Sheep and Wool Festival (September)
Essex Junction, VT
www.vermontsheep.org

Wool Festival at Taos (October)
Taos, NM
www.taoswoolfestival.org

FIBER ARTS INSTRUCTION

These craft schools and retreats offer classes in dyeing. Studying with many mentors will deepen your understanding of the craft.

Craft Schools

Harrisville Designs
Harrisville, NH
www.harrisville.com

Haystack Mountain School of Crafts
Deer Isle, ME
www.haystack-mtn.org

Peters Valley Craft Center
Layton, NJ
www.petersvalley.org

PRO Chemical & Dye
Falls River, MA
www.prochemical.com

Sievers School of Fiber Arts
Washington Island, WI
www.sieverschool.com

John C. Campbell Folk School
Brasstown, NC
www.folkschool.com

Retreats

Convergence
www.weavspindye.org

Fiber College
www.fibercollege.org

Mid Atlantic Fiber Association
conference: www.mafafiber.org

SOAR - Spin-Off Autumn Retreat
www.interweave.com/spin/events/soar/

ADDITIONAL READING

Blumenthal, Betsy, and Kreider, Kathryn. *Hands on Dyeing*. Loveland, CO: Interweave Press, 1988.

Brackman, Holly. *The Surface Designer's Handbook*. Loveland, CO: Interweave Press, 2006.

Delamare, Francois, and Guineau, Bernard. *Colors: The Story of Dyes and Pigments*. New York, NY: Harry N. Abrams, Inc., 1999.

Knutson, Linda. *Synthetic Dyes for Natural Fibers*. Loveland, CO: Interweave Press, 1986.

Lambert, Patricia; Staepelaere, Barbara; Fry, Mary G. *Color and Fiber*. West Chester, PA: Schiffer Press, 1986.

Lloyd, Lisa. *A Fine Fleece.* New York, NY: Potter Craft, 2008.

McCuin, Judith Mackenzie. *Teach Yourself VISUALLY Handspinning*. Hoboken, NJ: Wiley, 2007.

Menz, Deb. *Color in Spinning*. Loveland, CO: Interweave Press, 1998.

Menz, Deb. *Colorworks: The Crafter's Guide to Color*. Loveland, CO: Interweave Press, 2004.

Parks, Clara. *The Book of Yarn.* New York, NY: Potter Craft, 2007.

Rex, Susan. *Dyeing Wool and Protein Fibers*. Published by author, 2004.

Rivlin, Joseph. *The Dyeing of Textile Fibers: Theory and Practice*. 1992.

Roberts, Nancy. "Machine Knitting to Dye For." *Spin Off.* (Fall 2006), 60–65.

Seiff, Joanne. *Fiber Gathering: Knit, Crochet, Spin and Dye more than 25 Projects Inspired by America's Festivals.* Hoboken, NJ: Wiley, 2009.

Turner, Sharon. *Teach Yourself VISUALLY Knitting.* Hoboken, NJ: Wiley, 2006.

Vogel, Lynne, *The Twisted Sisters Sock Workbook*. Loveland, CO: Interweave Press, 2002.

Index

Want instruction in other topics?

Check out these

All designed for visual learners—just like you!

Read Less–Learn More®

Visual®

Teach Yourself **VISUALLY** Guitar
Charles Kim
0-7645-9642-X

Teach Yourself **VISUALLY** Knitting
Sharon Turner
0-7645-9640-3

Teach Yourself **VISUALLY** Windows XP 2nd Edition
Covers Windows XP Service Pack 2!
0-7645-7927-4

Look for these and other *Teach Yourself VISUALLY*™ titles wherever books are sold.

Visual®
An Imprint of ®WILEY
Now you know.

Wiley, the Wiley logo, the Visual logo, Read Less-Learn More, and Teach Yourself Visually are trademarks or registered trademarks of John Wiley & Sons, Inc. and/or its affiliates. All other trademarks are the property of their respective owners.